FRANCHISING

THE PROMISE AND THE PERIL

FRANCHISING
THE PROMISE AND THE PERIL

DENNIS L. FOSTER

Copyright © 2018 by Dennis L. Foster.

All rights reserved. No part of this publication may be reproduced or distributed in any form or by any means, or stored in a database or retrieval system, without prior written permission of the author.

CONTENTS

Preface: Why You Need to Read This Book — 1

1. The Changing Face of Franchising — 5
2. The Franchise Motive — 17
3. Who Makes a Good Franchisee? — 27
4. Inside the Franchise Relationship — 41
5. The Economics of Franchising — 57
6. Full and Accurate Disclosure — 73
7. Inside the Franchise Disclosure Document — 89
8. Inside the Franchise Decision — 109
9. A Franchisee's Rights and Obligations — 129
10. Why Franchise Disputes Happen — 141
11. Franchising and Technology — 153
12. Evaluating Franchise Offerings — 165
13. Inside the Franchise Agreement — 181
14. Getting Started in a Franchise Business — 197
15. Why Franchises Fail — 211
16. Franchising and the Future — 219

Epilog — 229

Appendix A: Sample Franchise Agreement — 231

Appendix B: Franchisee Resources — 243

PREFACE
Why You Need to Read this Book

The global economic landscape is presently undergoing a dramatic and sweeping transformation, shaped by a tsunami of financial, social, cultural, and demographic influences never before experienced in modern history.

For several decades, the franchise method of business has been an integral impetus of economic growth. Throughout most of that period, franchise businesses have ranked among the most reliable investments. On the average, three-fourths of franchise outlets remained open after five years, whereas about half of all other independently owned businesses failed, most within the first year.

Yet, in the last decade, record numbers of franchise outlets have closed, largely in response to rapidly changing consumer and business trends, shrinking disposable household income, and increasing stock market volatility. Nevertheless, franchising continues to out-perform most other business models, both as a contributor to economic growth and as an investment vehicle. Unfortunately, franchise-related fraud, feuding, and legal wrangling are also more prevalent than at any time since the first federal regulations were introduced in 1977.

Since 2005, new regulations have been enacted year by year on both state and federal levels, creating a new and complex regulatory environment today. Social and economic pressures ranging from massive migration to sharply changing consumer demographics are further altering the landscape. Increasing integration of technology with commerce will eventually replace the majority of the franchise workforce and automate virtually every aspect of doing business, from outlet management to product delivery. The internet and social media are changing the way franchises of all sizes market and sell their wares.

An unfavorable internet review or news event can propel an entire store chain into a sudden financial crisis, beyond the control of other outlet owners—a stomach-churning object in the food, a cup of hot coffee spilled in a lap, an organized protest over bathroom privileges. Changing cultural conditions, fashions, and consumer trends have also brought down some of the most successful franchise organizations, while making rising stars of new entrants into the field.

Despite the attention of government regulators and prosecuting attorneys, franchise feuds and frauds persist with increasing prevalence. Rapid over-expansion over the last two decades has stretched the resources of many of the world's leading franchisors beyond their limits. Vast chains once thought to be too big to fail are now closing hundreds and, in some cases, thousands of outlets, as share prices and retail sales fluctuate.

Nevertheless, franchising continues to be a powerful influence in the U.S. economy and, importantly, remains for the aspiring entrepreneur one of the most viable avenues to independent business ownership. However, the changing financial and regulatory landscape has redefined the very concept and execution of the franchise method of business, substantially transforming the relationship between franchisors and their franchisees and posing new challenges for both parties.

Franchising taps the entrepreneurial motives of individuals who seek financial independence, while generating an ongoing source of income to franchisors. From the franchisor's perspective, franchising offers to the corporation the ability to expand and diversify at reduced capital risk. From the franchisee's perspective, it offers self-esteem, an opportunity for self-management, and an asset of lasting value.

From a cultural perspective, the franchise phenomenon is both a driving force and a reflection of public tastes in food, fashion, and lodging. At its best, franchising exemplifies the free enterprise system's finest hour, a time for transforming simple ideas and bold ambitions into fulfilled dreams of personal enrichment and financial independence. At its worst, it is "vulture capitalism" run amok, in which every conceivable type of quick-buck scam and pyramid sales scheme is unleashed on an unsuspecting public.

Franchising: The Promise and the Peril is a sweeping, detailed analysis of the present state of the most powerful economic stimulant in the U.S. economy, from the new regulatory environment to the impact of technology and changing consumer, business, and economic trends. While exploring the benefits, components, and advantages of a franchise relationship, this book also exposes the increasing prevalence of rarely publicized feuds, frauds, and marketing miscues that confront prospective franchisees today.

Your life is the sum of the choices you have made in the past; your future will be the sum of the decisions, people, and strategic partnerships you choose today.

1
THE CHANGING FACE OF FRANCHISING

"The secret of business is to know something that nobody else knows."
Aristotle Onassis

> *"That place has been there for a while. It is like a city. They have Wi-Fi, organized disco nights, computers and video games, full plumbing with showers and toilets. On top of that, they've got Burger King, Pizza Hut, Green Bean, and Subway."*

So wrote the participant of a popular social media website. The author was a U.S. Marine, and his remarks described not some American small town or suburban neighborhood, but the largest military base in the Afghanistan war theater, Bagram Air Field.

Paris is widely regarded as the epicenter of fine cuisine and the home of the world's greatest chefs. Yet, the most crowded restaurants in the City of Lights are not Maxim's or *La Tour d'Argent*, where every roast duck has a registration number, but McDonald's, Wendy's, and Burger King. One of the city's most coveted hotel properties is the Paris Hilton, which features commanding, picture-perfect views of the Eiffel Tower.

In Beijing, the double-eaved Gate of Heavenly Peace, the largest of the four gates to the Imperial City, is guarded by two pairs of stone lions sculpted during the Ming Dynasty. On the opposite side of the Tianenmen Square sits the world's largest Kentucky Fried Chicken restaurant, opened in 1988. Almost thirty years later, Orkin established its first pest control franchise in the Chinese capital.

The first landmark viewed by visitors to King's Cross, the bustling tourism district of Sydney, Australia, is an iconic 20-story, flashing Coca-Cola logo. In the "land down under" are also hotels bearing the Hilton, Sheraton, and Holiday Inn logos, and fast-food outlets by Pizza Hut, McDonald's, Burger King, and KFC.

Hank Aaron, famous for his record-breaking 755 home runs during his illustrious 23-year baseball career, opened a pair of Church's Chicken franchise locations in 1995 and presently owns five units, in addition to twenty Popeye's Louisiana Kitchen and two Krispy Kreme outlets.

Hip-hop singer Kanye West purchased the rights to open ten Fatburger franchises, two of which are now open for business.

Airline passengers traveling to the remote South Pacific isle of Bora Bora arrive not on the island itself, but on an outlying *motu*, a coral formation rising above the surface of the ocean. From the airstrip, which was built by the U.S. military during World War II, passengers are ferried to the main island, where they are greeted by the yellow and black sign of a Hertz Rent-a-Car office.

These phenomena are symbolic of the pervasive cultural, as well as economic, impact of franchising in the modern world; for, each of these famous brand names is a franchise trademark.

An exhaustive list of franchise locations worldwide would require as many pages as this book. (The reason I know this is because I wrote *The Rating Guide to Franchises* and *The Encyclopedia of Franchising and Franchises*.)

From a cultural perspective, the franchise phenomenon is both a driving force and a reflection of public tastes in food, fashion, and lodging. In some way or another, franchising has managed to make its way into almost every corner of the earth. From Victoria, Canada to Victoria Falls, Zimbabwe, franchising has captured the public imagination and, in doing so, recruited to its ranks hundreds of thousands of aspiring small business owners.

To an attorney, a franchise is a lengthy contract; to an accountant, it is a financial relationship. To a banker, it is a relatively secure investment, but to a government regulator, it might be a red flag for consumer fraud.

The word franchise is derived from an Old French word, *franc*, meaning "free." Literally, a franchise is a right or privilege, as in the franchise to vote. As a business method, franchising means granting, for a fee, the right to use a particular trademark or to market an exclusive product. In a larger context, franchising has come to mean much more. A modern franchise entails an entire business system in which every aspect, from the architecture of the building to the color of the stationery, are planned in elaborate detail. In fact, many franchisors offer complete "turn key" store operations, fully stocked, equipped, and ready to open.

However, in an era of economic, technological, and social transition, it is no longer enough for a franchisor to provide a precooked business motif, a memorable brand, tools of the trade, and an operating manual. Franchisors today must be capable of providing competitive advantages and streamlined operations with the aid of advanced technology. Literally, a franchisor must be able to attract, motivate, and deliver customers to franchisees' doorsteps. In a period of fluctuating demand and economic uncertainty, financial advantages such as cooperative advertising, purchasing, and employee benefits are integral to survival, for franchisors and franchisees alike. The financial plight of every publicly traded franchising corporation literally hinges day-to-day on the throes of the stock market.

Despite these challenges, franchising continues to play an important role in the American economy. According to the Industry and Trade Administration of the U.S. Department of Commerce, over 75% of the franchises that were open five years ago are still in business today. In contrast, about half of all nonfranchise independent businesses eventually fail, most within the first two years.

Why have franchises been so successful over the last several decades? Studies show that people who own their own businesses are more devoted to their jobs than middle managers employed by large corporations. Franchisors benefit from the motivation and drive of their franchisees, while franchise owners benefit from the franchisor's trade secrets and industry knowledge. However, a franchise organization that lacks technological, marketing, and competitive advantages in today's rapidly evolving business environment is at risk of becoming stagnant. Too-rapid expansion has stretched many of the world's leading franchise chains beyond their limits, resulting in franchisee dissatisfaction, lack of uniform standards, and ongoing closures.

Today, identifying the signposts of obsolescence, stagnation, and internal turmoil is an indispensable process in making a franchise decision.

Franchising and the Law

At a legal conference I attended, an attorney proclaimed that franchising is nothing more than a legal entity. Indeed, a franchise is a complex legal relationship between two parties—a relationship that is further complicated by reams of federal and state regulations. However, without its various financial, marketing, and operating systems, franchising—and, thus, franchise law—would not exist. No contracts would be written, no regulations would be enacted, and no attorneys would be retained, if franchising was not first and foremost a business method based on the synergism between a successful *motif* and motivated entrepreneurs.

If a franchise relationship does not work for both parties, ultimately, it will work for neither. Unfortunately, not every franchise relationship has a happy ending, and much of the case law devoted to franchising involves unhappy franchisors or franchisees. Understanding the legal rights and obligations of both parties is a necessity in any franchise business.

Since 2005, a complex web of franchise regulations has been adopted by the U.S. Federal Trade Commission and various state governments, culminating in a set of new rules and exemptions implemented in 2015. When the federal government first began scrutinizing the offer and sale of franchises in June, 1977, more than half of the franchise opportunities that were advertised in the *Wall Street Journal* disappeared within the next thirty days. In this respect, regulation has had a favorable impact on the franchise industry, by protecting unwary investors against potential abuse. However, like many government regulations, the franchise rules are not always followed and are sometimes difficult to enforce.

Still, anyone who contemplates a franchise investment—or works for a franchisor or franchisee—needs to have a sound understanding of today's complex federal and state regulations affecting the offer, sale, operation, and termination of franchises. It is no less essential to be aware of litigation and court decisions that have altered and shaped the franchisor-franchisee relationship.

The Sociology of Franchising

While it is indisputable that franchise businesses reflect popular tastes and cultural trends, it is no less true that franchises also influence social behavior. The most manifest effect of franchising on modern society has been the widespread popularity of fast food. According to the National Restaurant Association, 90% of all meals taken in public in the United States are eaten at a fast-food restaurant. Predictably, the health and fitness industry has expanded almost in direct proportion to the popularity of "super sized" food and drink.

In food service and other major industries, such as lodging, automotive services, retail sales, and personal services, franchises have become so influential that they often dictate consumer trends, fashions, and pricing.

Major changes in consumption trends and customer demographics have an equally major impact on the franchise economy. As the population ages and new generations of consumers take center stage, their social behavior, food and fashion preferences, and spending ability are dictating the shape and fabric of the economic landscape.

The Physiology of Comfort

The need for comfort is deeply ingrained in all humans. We all seek out comfort where possible—physical comfort, emotional comfort, comfort in our jobs and in our social groups. However, comfort is not merely psychological. Research conducted by neuroscientists reveals that feelings of comfort coincide with increased electrochemical activity in certain regions of the brain. These impulses are triggered by sensory stimuli, such as scent, taste, sight, sound, and touch.

The scientists even found that the same areas of the brain become stimulated when a husband and wife hold hands. These emotional feelings are intrinsic values that inform animals how they are faring in their quest to survive. A positive signal indicates returning to a "comfort zone" that supports survival, whereas a negative signal indicates entering a "discomfort zone."

In humans, a basic component of the need for comfort is the security offered by familiarity. Franchise outlets cater to this emotion through the comfort of familiar products, surroundings, and standards of service. As franchising has spread, the security of sameness has become ingrained in the consumer consciousness. Few fears are more pronounced than the fear of the unknown. Who has not balked at turning into an unknown eatery by the highway, or driven past an anonymous motel in the hope of finding a recognizable brand name? Whose imagination has not conjured up nightmarish images of derelict washrooms or cockroach-infested rooms?

A basic law of marketing is that a customer's positive experience with one outlet reflects positively on other outlets, while a negative experience is a black mark on all.

The physiology of comfort is a fitting metaphor for the public's demonstrated preference for franchise outlets. The habit of returning to the "comfort zone" evolved in mammals as an adaptive benefit in the quest for survival. Similarly, humans patronize known business establishments, in part, from fear of the unknown. A franchise outlet attracts customers because it is a known commodity, where, in addition to familiarity and uniformity, patrons expect to find sanitation, efficiency, and friendly employees.

For this reason, franchise systems are often referred to as "cookie cutters," stamping out near-clones of their original flagship businesses, striving to create a security blanket of sameness. Consumers expect a Subway sandwich to taste the same in Victoria, Canada as in Victoria, Australia—or Victoria Falls, Zimbabwe, for that matter.

From chocolate chip cookies to computers, from togs to tacos, the most popular products are those that cater to the common denominator in public taste. Franchise outlets, with their uniform operating standards and cookie-cutter designs, are the very essence of that common denominator.

However, the lure of comfort zones and the security of sameness, by themselves, are not enough to ensure small business success. Unhealthy franchise systems cost a number of franchisees their investments, promote an unfavorable image of the franchise industry, and detract from investments being made in healthy systems. Over-expansion has become a serious problem in franchising today, resulting in dissatisfied franchisees, inability to enforce quality standards, and involuntary closures. As the "super consumer" generation of post-World II birth continues to age, consumer demand across many market sectors will inexorably decline — an event known by economists as the "Demographic Cliff."

Franchise chains, by virtue of their brand recognition, are subject to exaggerated effects resulting from everyday hazards. An unfavorable internet review or news event can inflict a sudden financial crisis on an entire chain, beyond the control of outlet owners — a stomach-churning object in the food, a cup of hot coffee spilled in a lap, an organized protest over bathroom privileges.

When a customer of a Wendy's fast-food outlet in Fresno, California claimed to have found a severed human finger in a container of chili, the franchisor suffered $250 million in losses, as wary consumers avoided the chain's outlets. The finger turned out to have been planted by the accuser, but other highly publicized incidents have been substantiated, including a syringe found in a Burger King sandwich in Switzerland; a Band-Aid in a container of French Fries at a McDonald's outlet in Canada; and an intact, deep-fried chicken's head — complete with beak, eyes, and comb — at an outlet in Virginia.

Besides news events, changing cultural conditions, fashions, and consumer trends have also brought down some of the most successful franchise organizations, while making rising stars of new entrants into the field. With the rise of the fitness fad, restaurants specializing in "healthy" menu options began to proliferate, but, as the fad began to wane, inevitably declined in popularity. Mobile diaper laundering vans, often seen navigating city and suburban streets in the 1950s, have all but disappeared from the public consciousness. However, public preferences fluctuate over time, and it is not unreasonable to anticipate that "fitness foods" and infant-related services could once again become profitable commodities at some point in the future.

Franchising and the Economy

Because of the successful track record of franchise businesses, some major corporations involved in franchising are highly prized as investments. At various times, the shares of McDonald's, Coca-Cola, Hilton, and other franchisors have soared in value. In addition, absentee investment in franchise businesses has become a virtual mainstay of venture capital groups and fund managers. Multi-unit franchises, area franchising, and international expansion are currently among the most sought-after investment options.

The University of New Hampshire's Rosenberg Center compiles an index that tracks the market performance of the top 50 U.S. public franchisors every quarter. Over 98% of the market capitalization of corporations involved in the business of franchising is represented by the Rosenberg Center Franchise (RCF) 50 Index. This composite index of franchisors has consistently outperformed the Standard and Poor's index of the 500 leading stocks.

Forecasting the future is more difficult than analyzing the past. Nevertheless, the health of a franchise system is defined to a large extent by its financial condition. McDonald's stock first appeared on the New York Stock Exchange on April 15, 1965 at about seventeen times the company's earnings for the prior year. Within weeks, the price soared from $22.50 to $49.00 a share. As of this writing, McDonald's stock is trading at about $165.00 per share, having soared by $50 per share in two years. However, in 2012, McDonald's stock was downgraded from a "buy" (a recommendation for investors to invest) to a "neutral rating."

This type of move is a daily occurrence on Wall Street, but for the iconic franchisor, it was an indicator of a more deeply rooted issue. The McDonald's first-quarter financial results had shown a 1.2% decrease in U.S. sales and a one percent drop globally. In April 2016, McDonald's launched a system-wide "turnaround" plan, which included introducing new menu items and closing faltering outlets.

With the high success rate of franchise outlets, lenders have traditionally been more willing to finance franchise start-ups than other small businesses. Commercial finance companies, venture capitalists, profit sharing funds, and banks provide over two thirds of the total capitalization of retail franchises.

As of this writing, franchises account for about $3.1 trillion in gross annual sales. Nearly 900,000 franchise outlets in the United States employ over seven percent of all nonagricultural employees. In aggregate, more than nine million Americans are currently employed by franchise outlets. One of every twelve retail establishments is a franchise business. The number of people who are actively interested in investing in a franchise opportunity has never been greater. A new franchise outlet is opened every eight minutes of every business day.

It should not be overlooked that for every ten new outlets that open each year, eight existing outlets close. Still, the percentage of franchise outlets that are terminated, sold, transferred, or cease to operate is lower than the failure rate of other, comparable small businesses. Overall, the lowest performing 25% of all franchise chains account for over 60% of all annual outlet closures.

According to the U.S. Department of Commerce, franchising is the average American's most viable means of owning a business. Business owners undeniably sacrifice some measure of independence to become franchisees. They also sacrifice a percentage of their income in the form of a royalty on all gross revenues. The payoff is that a franchise is more likely to succeed than other comparable businesses.

Nevertheless, in an era of constantly changing consumer and business trends, household income, and stock market volatility, record numbers of franchise outlets continue to close each year. Moreover, as franchising has spread in popularity, franchise-related fraud, feuding, and legal wrangling have taken center stage.

Now, more than at any previous time in the history of the American economy, prospective franchisees and investors face a morass of economic, regulatory, financial, and cultural challenges, any one of which can make the difference between success and failure.

However, franchising is about more than retail sales, employment, and small business survival. It is also about self-fulfillment, personal expression, and creativity. A person who invests in a franchise does not just buy himself or herself a job. Franchisees are people motivated by accomplishment and driven by a dream—of self-management, financial independence, and personal enrichment.

Though motivation is an essential ingredient of being an entrepreneur, navigating today's complex franchise landscape requires large doses of diligence, analysis, perseverance, and, especially, inside knowledge. The information in the following chapters is written to help readers sort out the facts about franchising in today's complex and rapidly changing economic and regulatory environment, and to distinguish the signposts of success from the danger signals of fraud or failure.

Leading Franchise Categories

	Outlets	Revenues (Billions)	Employees
Fast Food	162,200	$244	3,433,200
Personal Services	117,100	$102	716,100
Retail Goods	104,100	$46	537,300
Business Services	99,600	$59	1,014,100
Real Estate	93,100	$57	325,000
Commercial Services	65,500	$60	385,400
Food/Groceries	64,400	$45	533,100
Full Service Restaurants	39,500	$69	1,147,400
Automotive	32,400	$43	197,200
Lodging	27,800	$94	765,400

2
THE FRANCHISE MOTIVE

"Chase the vision, not the money; the money will end up following you."
                                                    Tony Hsieh

The rhinoceros is one of the largest and most formidable mammals on the African continent. It is rarely seen except in the company of one of the smallest and least imposing species, the oxpecker. The rhino grazes on the African savanna and takes shelter in dense thickets of thorny brush, which is also the habitat of bloodsucking ticks. The oxpecker lives most its life perched atop the rhino's back, dining on ticks, flies, and other parasites. With poor vision, the rhino relies instead on the oxpecker's hisses and caws to raise the alarm against approaching predators. Though both animals could survive without the other, each enjoys a better life as a result of their mutually beneficial relationship.

This type of behavior is a classic *symbiotic* relationship—one in which each party is dependent on the other for survival. A biological relationship in which both organisms thrive as a result of their interdependence is called mutualism. More than any other factor, it is the mutualism of a franchise relationship, the synergistic effect created by the contributions of both parties, that underlies the competitive advantages of franchising.

In the most basic sense, a "franchise" is a right or privilege to conduct a particular business using a specified trade name. Trade secrets and a packaged business format are usually part of the deal. The "franchisor" is the company that offers the franchise to others. The person who buys a franchise from a franchisor is the "franchisee."

Franchising enables a franchisor to enter new geographical markets quickly and expand its sources of revenue. People who invest in a franchise expect to obtain a ready-made format for a business and improved odds for survival.

For the benefits and advantages of a franchise license, the franchisee pays an initial fee, an ongoing royalty, or both. In this way, the franchisor receives a continuous supply of working capital to expand and develop the organization.

The most fundamental type of franchise is a license to use a distinctive trademark or to market an exclusive product. A sales territory is often included with the license. For instance, during the Civil War era, a Singer franchisee obtained a license to sell sewing machines within an established geographic area. This type of arrangement is referred to as a trademark or distributor franchise.

Coca-Cola is the most famous example of a trademark franchise. Throughout the company's history, the recipe for the Coca-Cola syrup presumably remained a carefully guarded secret passed between family members. The soft drink is produced by independent bottling companies operated under franchise agreements with the franchisor, nicknamed "Big Coke" by franchisees. A hallmark of the Coca-Cola franchise is an exclusive territory granted to the franchisee "in perpetuity."

Today, with $44 billion in annual sales, the Coca-Cola franchise empire is the largest beverage company and one of the most influential business organizations in the world. Sixty percent of the company's sales originate from overseas franchises. "Big Coke" has even received applications for franchises on the moon.

The basis of the Coca-Cola franchise is its famous trade name and the secret recipe for the syrup. However, a franchise does not have to have a secret recipe, or even an exclusive product, to be successful. Most modern franchises are based on the "cookie-cutter" concept, known more formally as business format franchising.

Business Format Franchising

Three elements are integral to franchise success: a refined business format, a recognizable trade name, and an ongoing support system for franchisees. Alone, each of these components have a tangible value, yet without one other element they would not be enough to create a successful franchise program.

That element is know-how. A successful franchisor knows what to do—and what not to do—to succeed in a small business.

Aaron Copeland's story, which remains both inspirational and instructive today, illustrates this principle. Aaron was a 16-year-old grocery clerk in New Orleans when his brother Gilbert offered him a job in a doughnut shop. Alvin set out to learn the fast food business and, in 1966, decided to start his own fried chicken restaurant. He tried and failed with two different restaurants, before finally capturing the right combination of food preparation and restaurant location.

Aaron named the fast-food stand Popeyes (no apostrophe) Mighty Good Fried Chicken. He insisted the outlet was named after Popeye Doyle, the main character in the motion picture *The French Connection*, not the brawling, spinach-guzzling Popeye the Sailor cartoon character.

Copeland was fond of telling anyone who asked that the eatery's name came about because he "couldn't afford an apostrophe." Later, Copeland obtained a license from King Features to use the name and image of the Popeye cartoon character, resulting at last in an apostrophe.

Within ten months after his first outlet opened, Copeland was earning $5,000 a week, prompting the enterprising youth to open a second outlet across town. Over the next two years, he opened another 22 restaurants, all financed with his own earnings. By 1986, another 500 outlets had opened.

Unfortunately, the chain eventually fell victim to overly rapid expansion, stretching the franchisor beyond its limits. In 1992, Copeland Enterprises, after defaulting on $391 million in debts, filed for bankruptcy protection. As a result, a new court-appointed entity, America's Favorite Chicken Company, Inc. (AFC), emerged as the new parent company for Popeye's, as well as the Church's Fried Chicken organization. In 2004, AFC sold its interest in the Church's chain but retained control of the Popeye's franchise.

The franchisor's relationship with King Features was terminated two years later, ending the use of the Popeye cartoon character. Today, Popeye's Louisiana Kitchen, as the franchise is now branded, is a multinational chain with more than 2,500 outlets in 40 U.S. states and 30 countries.

As Popeye's tumultuous history demonstrates, the early failures and diverse problems encountered by the franchisor in developing the business are invaluable lessons to franchisees opening new outlets. One important benefit of investing in a franchise is avoiding the trial-and-error pitfalls that doom most small businesses.

However, a franchise chain does not become successful just by providing franchisees with know-how, a business format, and a well-known product to sell. Without the ambition, drive, and entrepreneurial spirit of franchisees, no franchise chain can hope to succeed over the long haul.

Franchising and the Entrepreneur

Mark Cafua was just five years old when his Portuguese parents decided to open a Dunkin' Donuts franchise outlet. He spent his school years working in the shop. His most important education was the advice he received from his parents' employees. Now in his forties, Mark and his two brothers operate 300 Dunkin' Donuts shops bringing in over $250 million a year.

As Cafua's American success story demonstrates, it is possible for a franchisee to become quite wealthy. In fact, some franchisees have become more successful than their franchisors. However, most people purchase franchise businesses to pursue a personal dream of independence and self-management. According to a 2015 survey of franchisee satisfaction across all market sectors, 78% of existing franchisees believe their investments have met or exceeded their expectations. In the same survey, 74% also indicated that, if given the same opportunity, they would invest in the same franchise again.

As this survey reveals, a key factor in the success of any franchise is the franchisee's entrepreneurial spirit.

When a franchise company recruits franchisees to join its organization, the applicant's personal ambition is a key consideration. As a rule, people who own their own businesses are more dedicated to success than middle managers or department heads of corporations. That dedication translates into more satisfied customers and increased revenue for the outlet. Franchising works for franchisors not just because it works for franchisees, but because franchisees also work for it.

Someone who buys a franchise expects to receive a business package that would otherwise take years to develop and refine. Franchisees also expect to benefit from a strengthened ability to compete in the marketplace. Contributions collected from all the licensed outlets can be used to finance major advertising campaigns that an independent operator could never afford.

From these campaigns, each franchisee should be able to derive the image and marketing power of an industry giant. In addition, a franchisee expects to obtain collective purchasing power, enabling the business to obtain equipment, goods, and services at reduced cost. Anyone who invests in a franchise expects to receive the benefit of the franchisor's know-how to avoid the costly mistakes that doom most small-time operators.

But what about the franchisor? Why should a successful company be willing to hand out its trade secrets and brand recognition to put small-time operators in business for themselves?

The history of 7-Eleven Stores provides a clue. The chain's parent company, The Southland Corporation began in 1927 as an ice vending business. When one of the ice dock managers began offering customers bread, milk, and eggs, in addition to ice, the firm entered the convenience retailing industry. In 1964, Southland acquired a chain of franchised stores in California. Since then, the company has sold more than 60,000 new 7-Eleven franchises worldwide and is the third largest global franchise chain.

A franchisor's motives are not much different from those of a franchisee. By franchising, a company gains the potential of building a business empire worth many millions from a relatively small investment. A franchisor receives ongoing royalty payments from the outlet's combined gross sales, but may also produce revenues from selling supplies or equipment to franchisees.

The Regulatory Atmosphere

Despite the influence of franchising in the economy today, buying a franchise, like all investments, is a potentially risky venture. Virtually anyone with an idea for sale, where proved or not, is able to sell so-called "franchises" to eager, unsuspecting buyers. Many of these buyers end up with little more than empty pockets and broken dreams.

Consider the case of Roberto Dominguez, who immigrated to the United States in 2012. Through hard work and frugal living, he had saved enough money to purchase a franchise to operate a commercial janitorial service. The franchisor had promised to provide training, supplies, and a steady base of clients.

After two years, despite working 90 hours per week, Roberto was unable to pay his bills and forced to mortgage his home to cover the expenses of the business. Instead of an American Dream of financial opportunity and independence, Roberto ended up, for tens of thousands of dollars, buying himself a bad job that didn't even allow him to break even.

The federal government has attempted to curb such abuses since 1980, when it first stepped in to by regulate the offer and sale of franchises. Since then, increasing regulation at the state and federal level has occurred year by year.

In today's strict regulatory environment, franchisors must comply with a long list of disclosures and requirements. The Federal Trade Commission (FTC) first introduced extensive franchise reform in 1980. The FTC regulations were modeled after the 1971 California Franchise Investment Protection Law, which in turn was adapted from a paper created by a convention of Midwestern securities commissioners. Since 2005, encompassing regulations have continued to be enacted, while exemptions to existing regulations have also been adopted, creating a new and complex regulatory environment today.

The first of the "full and accurate disclosure" laws governing franchise opportunities was passed by the California legislature in 1971. Today, fifteen states have similar laws on their books. These laws range from requiring filing of an annual notice to a full-fledged review of a franchise registration application and a renewal registration application on an annual basis. The states that have enacted laws regulating the offer and sale of franchises are California, Hawaii, Illinois, Indiana, Maryland, Minnesota, New York, North Dakota, Oregon, Rhode Island, South Dakota, Virginia, Washington, and Wisconsin. Oregon authorities require disclosure, but not registration.

In the Franchise Disclosure Document (FDD) a franchisor must inform prospective franchisees about the background of those offering the franchise and the mutual obligations created by the franchise agreement. In some states, this information must be filed with an agency responsible for monitoring franchises. A state regulator may have to approve the offering before it can be promoted to prospective franchise buyers.

The Federal Franchise Rule requires franchisors in every state to provide a FDD to prospective franchisees before the contract can be signed or any payment can be made. If a franchise salesman asks a prospect to pay a deposit before the prescribed time period has elapsed—and most assuredly, there are some who do—it may be in violation of state or federal law.

In most states with specific franchise laws, franchisors must also comply with the opinions of state-employed regulators. Such authorities have almost unlimited power over who may and may not do business in their states. However, certain state franchise laws now provide exemptions from registration based on a franchisor's high net worth and/or operational experience.

Even in an unregulated state, a franchisor must follow the FTC's requirements for full and accurate disclosure in the form of a Franchise Disclosure Document. Legally, a potential buyer may not be coerced, persuaded, or tricked into signing until all the facts have been disclosed and clarified.

Other regulations affect what happens after a contract is signed. For example, Iowa legislators enacted the Franchise Relationship Law, which gives franchisees specific rights above and beyond those stated in a franchise agreement. Among other things, the Iowa law requires franchisors to permit franchisees to transfer their ownership and restricts a franchisor's ability to locate additional outlets within an existing franchisee's market area. After the Iowa law was enacted, eighteen other states proposed similar legislation.

The International Franchise Association, a prominent lobbying group for franchisors, has routinely opposed the adoption of new, more restrictive state and federal laws regulating franchisors. The IFA's position is that complying with regulations is costly to franchisors and reduces profits. People in favor of more restrictive regulations include unhappy investors who have lost money or businesses to unscrupulous franchisors, or have become embroiled in feuds.

Clearly, a majority of franchisors are honest; a relatively small percentage of the franchise investments that are made each year result in complaints or lawsuits. Still, the number of disputes, abuses, and outright frauds continues to increase every year. Some legislators and attorneys argue that the present regulations do not go far enough to protect investors. Others insist that voluntary self-regulation of the franchising industry is preferable to enacting new laws.

Rules and regulations are but one aspect of a franchise investment. The remaining chapters of this book explore the psychological, ethical, sociological, legal, and financial forces that make franchising work, while exploring the subtle, sometimes volatile, franchisor-franchisee relationship.

3
WHO MAKES A GOOD FRANCHISEE?

"Your work is going to fill a large part of your life, and the only way to be truly satisfied is to do what you believe is great work. And the only way to do great work is to love what you do."
                                                            Steve Jobs

Statistics suggesting that franchising is the average person's most viable method of independent business ownership are widely publicized. Nevertheless, not everyone who intends to go into business for himself or herself is a suitable candidate for a franchise business. The traits that characterize successful franchisees vary depending on the business or industry, market, and, certainly, the structure and personality of the franchising company itself.

Certain qualities distinguish best-odds franchise operators from other small business owners in terms of personality traits, thinking styles, and learning styles.

Financial considerations aside, a savvy franchisor devotes considerable efforts to ascertaining the behavioral attributes that contribute to success, not only in relation to operating a business, but, more specifically, with a focus on the franchisor's own business format and market. For example, the owner of an exercise gym might be expected to have different motives and personality traits than the operator of an automobile oil change franchise. Despite these differences, all prospective franchisees can be evaluated with regard to traits shared by others already succeeding in the marketplace.

There are numerous personality and motivational models and theories, each offering a different perspective.

Psychometrics

An individual's knowledge, abilities, attitudes, and personality traits can be evaluated by means of psychometrics. Questionnaires designed to elicit pertinent information about a job applicant are examples of psychometric tools. Increasingly, franchisor are also employing psychometric evaluation to qualify prospective franchisees. However, the same principles used to evaluate others can also be used for self-assessment.

The science of psychometrics is rooted in ancient Greece. In 370 BC, Hippocrates, commonly regarded as the "father of modern medicine," defined four basic personality traits, or "temperaments:" cheerful, somber, enthusiastic, and calm. Over the centuries, numerous theorists drew inspiration and guidance from the ancient Four Temperaments model. One of the most influential was Carl Jung, whose book *Psychological Types*, published in 1921, broke new ground in clinical psychology and analysis. Like his collaborator, Sigmund Freud, Jung was devoted to discovering, developing, and enhancing knowledge about the mind and its underlying mechanisms. Carl Jung's structuring of "psychological types" continues to provide the basis for many of the psychometric systems and tools in use today.

Jung's theories are based on the idea that the mind continuously operates on two levels at the same time: the conscious and the unconscious. An individual's psyche, defined by Jung as the "whole being," consists of both processes. The psychologist believed that the conscious and unconscious states are self-balancing. If the conscious self becomes dominant or extreme, the unconscious reacts in such a way as to maintain the balance.

Jung divided psychic energy into two basic "general attitude types:" introverted and extroverted, both of which are present in every person in different degrees. No one is purely extraverted or introverted, but, for the most part, a reasonably well-balanced mixture of both types.

Drawing inspiration from Hippocrates, Aristotle, and others, Jung defined four functions of the human mind: thinking, feeling, sensation, and intuition. The first two are the functions that enable us to decide and judge, the so-called rational functions. The other two, which Jung considered the irrational functions, enable us to gather information and perceive.

The thinking function consists of the rational process of understanding reality and cause-effect relationships in a logical and analytical way. It is systematic, evaluates truth, and is objective, based on the individual's relative intelligence and comprehension. The feeling function forms judgments on a purely subjective basis. Invoking sentimentality, it is responsible for forming opinions, defining right and wrong behavior, and separating acceptable acts from unacceptable ones.

The sensation function translates signals from the senses into factual data. No judgement or interpretation of right or wrong, good or bad, causes, themes, or related concepts occurs. The intuition function translates facts and details into larger conceptual ideas, imaginings, and theories, without analyzing them.

In Jung's structure, thinking and feeling are opposites, as are sensation and intuition.

By dividing his four functions of the human psyche into extroverted and introverted attitudes, the psychologist arrived at eight psychological types:

Extraverted Thinking: Analytical and strategic, extraverted thinking is responsible for formulating and implementing plans, and organizing others.

Introverted Thinking: Contemplative, discovering, and theoretical, introverted thinking seeks self-knowledge.

Extraverted Feeling: Sociable and sentimental, extraverted feeling seeks personal and social success.

Introverted Feeling: Inaccessible, enigmatic, and self-contained, introverted feeling seeks inner intensity.

Extraverted Sensation: Practical and hands-on, extraverted sensation is pleasure-seeking and obstinate.

Introverted Sensation: Intense, obsessive, and detached, introverted sensation strives to be a connoisseur or expert.

Extraverted Intuition: Adventurous and innovative, extraverted intuition seeks novelty and proposes change.

Introverted Intuition: Idealistic, visionary, and esoteric, introverted intuition embraces the mystical and seeks to be aloof.

Though the behavioral traits described in these classifications may seem obvious, Jung's eight psychological types formed the basis for modern psychometrics. Everyone exhibits these traits at various times, in varying degrees. Identifying and measuring their respective influence has become a common way of evaluating a person's suitability for a particular employment scenario. In terms of franchising, the measurements focus on the following key skill sets:

- Self-understanding and development
- Understanding and developing others
- Understanding what motivates others
- Understanding others' strengths and weaknesses

- ☐ Ability to work in a team
- ☐ Agreeing to and allocating of tasks and responsibilities
- ☐ Agreeing to and assigning of roles for oneself as well as others

Although many people would like to be their own boss, it is clear that not everyone who wants to own a business would make a successful franchisee. Anyone who enters into a franchise agreement sacrifices some measure of entrepreneurial independence. Prospective franchisees who resist the concept of obeying a laundry list of mandatory policies and procedures, ultimately will have an unhappy experience in franchising.

Investigating, evaluating, investing in, and undertaking a franchise business are not exclusively rational considerations. There is an emotional side to every important decision, particularly one that will so profoundly affect one's life, career, and well-being. Yet, if you are someone considering a franchise investment, it is important to balance that emotional part against the purely rational aspects of where you are now, where you want to be in the future, and how you are going to get there.

No matter how logical a franchise choice might seem initially, unless the prospective franchisee truly loves the work, his or her commitment to success will be something less than total. In a franchise, nothing less than total commitment will do. In any line of business, the perfect franchise is the one that best matches your personality, desires, abilities, and budget.

Most people considering a franchise investment ask the obvious question: Would the business be right for me? However, it is equally important to ask: Is franchising right for me? Despite the impressive track record of franchises, not everyone who would like to own a franchise outlet has the right personality traits and skill sets to succeed in the business.

Before embarking on this adventurous and potentially risky undertaking, it is important to devote some serious thought and time to self-evaluation.

Exactly why should you consider franchising, rather than making a go of it on your own? After all, 20% of independent business owners succeed on their own, and perhaps you might be one of them. Then again, maybe your personality, aptitudes, and skills more closely match those of America's 800,000 franchise owners.

After a franchise agreement is signed, the franchisor will call many of the shots. Can you live with the obligations and restrictions of a franchise agreement? A franchisor will provide training and guidance, but you will also be saddled with a staggering array of mandatory policies and procedures. Ultimately, the franchisee, as the owner of the business, is accountable for its success or failure.

Who Owns a Business?

Now, perhaps more than at any time in the last century, the characteristics of business owners—and the economic and business environment in which they operate—are continually changing. Indisputably, small business owners and entrepreneurs make important contributions to business creation and growth in the American economy. According to the U.S. Small Business Administration, understanding the characteristics of business owners is important in measuring the overall economic well-being of the economy.

According to demographics compiled by the U.S. Census Bureau, a typical small business owner is age 50 or older, married, and a military veteran, with a bachelor's degree or higher education. Most business owners are located in metropolitan areas and own their own homes. Women own just over 35% of small businesses. About 15% are owned by minorities, with Asian, Black, and Hispanics making up the largest share.

Who Invests in a Franchise?

The median age for franchise owners is 45 to 54 years, with the majority of these business owners residing in California (37,238 units) and Texas (28,094). The states with the fewest number of franchisees are Alaska (695 units) and Vermont (619 units).

Certain industries are more popular than others. Fast food outlets, lodging establishments, and business-related services enjoy a larger market share, while outlets specializing in DVD rentals, home security, and party-related goods have the lowest number of outlets.

Individuals possessing a Bachelor's degree own 44% of the franchise market share and 19% of owners hold an advanced degree. Military veterans make up 12% of ownership. About 72% of all franchises outlets are owned by males. Multi-unit operators own 54% of all outlets. Within this group 52% own two franchises, and 17% own three. Nearly 90% of multi-unit owners are devoted to one brand.

The average start up investment is $520,000. Franchise operators over 55 years old represent 28% of the industry, while 12% are represented by individuals 34 years old or younger. Twenty percent own their business for more than tem years, 18% own their business for six to nine years, and 32% for two to five years. For 30% of franchisees, the length of ownership is less than two years.

One in five franchise owners work 60 hours or more per week. In all, 70% work more than 40 hours per week.
Male franchisees earn an average of $73,261 per year, while females earn $54,408 per year.

Eleven percent of franchise owners make over $150,000 per year.

Demographic Characteristics of Business Owners and Employees

	Total Employed	Owners	Employees
Age			
Under 35	35.1	15.6	38.3
35 to 49	32.4	32.7	32.3
50 to 88	32.5	51.7	29.3
Gender			
Male	54.4	64.6	52.7
Female	45.6	35.4	47.3
Race			
Non-Minority	80.4	85.9	79.5
Minority	19.6	14.1	20.5
Ethnicity			
Hispanic	15.9	10.6	16.7
Non-Hispanic	84.1	89.4	83.3
Veteran Status			
Veteran	6.0	9.0	5.5
Non-Veteran	94.0	91.0	94.5
Marital Status			
Married	53.8	66.3	51.7
Not Married	46.2	33.7	48.3
Education			
High School	33.6	28.0	34.6
Some College	35.7	32.8	36.2
College Degree	30.6	39.2	29.2
Homeowner			
Yes	67.1	77.5	65.4
No	32.9	22.5	34.6
Location			
Urban	80.8	79.1	81.1
Other	19.2	20.9	18.9

Source: U.S. Small Business Administration

Traits of Successful Franchisees

Based on studies of franchisee motivation, for more than one half of the applicants, the main reason for investing in a franchise is the desire to be one's own boss. People who acquire franchises, whether male or female, seek an opportunity for self-management and self-expression. Some are individuals who were frustrated with their former jobs and were on the lookout for independence. Others pursued a personal dream to own a successful business.

Many franchisees actually sacrifice a portion of their earnings potential as wage earners for the opportunity to own their own businesses. Some of the franchisees studied enjoyed satisfactory incomes before setting out on their own, yet decided on franchise opportunities that they knew would not earn them as good a living as their former occupations.

A common conception is that everyone in the workforce would prefer to be his or her own boss. However, many people would rather not experience the headaches that come with the territory. Every platoon has only one commanding officer but many rank-and-file soldiers who would rather follow orders than formulate them. A successful franchisee is someone who is capable of leading others, but is also agreeable to following the objectives and general guidance of a superior.

A prominent reason people invest in franchises is the quest for financial growth and, ultimately, wealth. Many franchises are purchased strictly for investment purposes, based on their speculative value.

Everyone who goes into business for himself or herself is pursuing a dream of financial independence and security. Someone who invests in a franchise most likely expects more from life than the seeming drudgery of a wage-earning career. He or she has a high level of ambition and an irrepressible belief that the rewards outweigh the risks. So, although money may not be the number-one consideration in the minds of franchise owners, it's still high on the list.

People also invest in franchises from a desire to be a winner. Most of us have a longing for a positive self-image and heightened self-esteem. Franchisees enjoy the identity of success and, through their tie-in with a large organization, the industry dominance that accompanies the business. Many people buy franchises in the hope that their franchisor's successful image will rubs off on their own businesses.

Another reason people invest in franchises is to obtain training and guidance from an experienced industry insider. Franchisees are more likely than other entrepreneurs to recognize their own limitations. They know it takes a broad range of insights and skills to develop a successful business. After all, who among us is a competent chief executive, industry expert, creative advertising executive, skilled financial officer, and experienced personnel director, all rolled into in one?

Franchise buyers seek know-how and support in the crucial aspects of running a business, especially advertising, accounting, and industry practices. I once spoke with the owner of three hairstyling franchises, who reported that what he primarily sought was "a big head start" (pun unintended). Asked why he invested in a franchise rather than simply opening his own hair salons, the entrepreneur responded: "I planned to open these salons anyway. With a franchise, I have at least a three-year head start."

From the owner's perspective, a franchise business can be viewed as an asset of lasting value. Franchise outlets are commonly resold to other, qualified, often for a substantial profit. Most independently owned small businesses are fortunate to survive only five years, whereas a franchise agreement has an average term of ten years and is almost always renewable.

Another significant statistic is the increase in the number of women who own franchises, an indication of the growing importance of female entrepreneurs in franchising.

No matter what your gender, if you are motivated to be your own boss, want to build a business that will have a lasting value, and are willing to sacrifice a portion of your independence to obtain a competitive edge, you may be a prime candidate for a franchise investment.

However, even with a franchisor's help, starting a business is not exactly a pleasure cruise. No one should contemplate a franchise investment without taking inventory of the personal work skills and competency that contribute to success.

Skills and competency self-assessment

__ Using and developing your knowledge.
__ Researching, investigating, and problem-solving.
__ Communicating outwardly: face-to-face, phone, email, social media, etc.
__ Listening and interpretation, establishing rapport, understanding needs.
__ Developing solutions and agreeing things with people.
__ Financial understanding and commercial ability.
__ Speaking and presenting to groups.
__ Helping or coaching or teaching or training others.
__ Using information and communications technology
__ Technical appreciation and use of equipment, tools, or machinery.
__ Understanding and making the most of relationships with people and groups.
__ Competitor/industry awareness and consideration of these factors in planning, decision-making, etc.
__ Taking initiative and responsibility, e.g., decision-making, project management, running meetings.
__ Visioning, creating, and inspiring others with my ideas.
__ Managing time, planning, being effective, efficient, productive, and reliable.
__ Appreciating/applying social responsibility, sustainability, humanity and ethical considerations.
__ Striving for personal development.
__ Taking personal responsibility to resolve problems, even those not of my own making.
__ Understanding the way people really feel.
__ Developing positive relationships.

___ Keeping focused and productive, reliable and dependable.
___ Planning how to achieve my work and personal goals.
___ Managing stress and conflict.
___ Contributing positively to team/company morale and spirit.
___ Seeking and picking up responsibility that I see waiting to be filled.
___ Working positively as a member of a team.
___ Having compassion and care for others.
___ Using integrity and ethics in my judgment about work and organizational issues.

4
INSIDE THE FRANCHISE RELATIONSHIP

"Rank does not confer privilege or give power. It imposes responsibility."
Peter Drucker

Aside from sports franchises, there is little conceptual difference in the public consciousness between the words "franchise" and "chain." In fact, to the average consumer, as well as to many investors, the distinction between company-owned outlets and franchise businesses is largely invisible. KFC, for example, is more likely to be equated with a "fast food chain" than a franchise organization.

Most people neither know nor care that many of the best known businesses housed in their local shopping malls and strip centers are operated by independent owners under franchise licenses. The typical food and beverage consumer does not distinguish between Subway, which is a franchise business, and Starbuck's, which is not. In some respects, it is that very public perception (or lack of perception) that provides the franchise establishment with the same competitive advantages of a chain store.

A business format franchise can be viewed from three different perspectives, each with its own criteria deserving special consideration: legal, operational, and strategic. The legal perspective is based on federal regulations, state laws, and court decisions. However, the aspiring entrepreneur is equally, if not more, interested in the operational anatomy of a franchise business, while an investor or financier is likely to focus on the strategic aspects.

Legal Definition

The term "franchise" appears in a number of federal regulations and state laws. However, the definition may vary depending on the specific regulation or law. The federal definition of a franchise is found in Federal Trade Commission Amended Franchise Rule 16 C.F.R., Part 436, as follows:

> *"The term "franchise" means any continuing commercial relationship created by any arrangement or arrangements whereby...a person offers, sells, or distributes to any person...goods, commodities, or services which are: (1) identified by a trademark, service mark, trade name, advertising or other commercial symbol...or (2) directly or indirectly required or advised to meet the quality standards prescribed by another person where the franchisee operates under a name using the trademark, service mark, trade name, advertising or other commercial symbol..."*

The Trademark Element

In plain English, the first component is a trademark, logo, or trade name that is owned by the franchisor and licensed to the franchisee. For example, a franchisee who acquires a Hilton franchise receives the right to put up the Hilton sign on the hotel. Likewise, other franchisees receive the right to operate under such well known trade names as McDonald's, 7-Eleven, or Hertz.

To fall under federal jurisdiction, the business must be substantially associated with the franchisor's trademark or other commercial symbol. This association usually takes the form of a license to use the franchisor's name. Because franchise laws were enacted to remedy perceived abuses in the treatment of franchisees, courts will often interpret those laws broadly.

The "trademark element" is based on the franchisee's right to operate a business that is "identified or associated with the franchisor's trademark, or to offer, sell, or distribute goods, services, or commodities that are identified or associated with the franchisor's trademark." The term "trademark" in the Amended FTC Rule covers not only registered trademarks, but any service mark, trade name, or other advertising or commercial symbol. The franchisor does not have to actually own the trademark, but must have the right to license the use of the trademark to others.

The FTC considers that the right to use the franchisor's trademark is an integral component of franchising. In fact, a supplier can become exempt from federal regulations by explicitly prohibiting distributors from using its trademark. However, by permitting a distributor or retailer to use its trademark, a supplier legally engages in a franchise relationship—at least, according to the letter of the Amended Franchise Rule.

The Significant Control or Assistance Element

The second legal component of a franchise is a set of quality standards. For example, a fast-food franchisor usually sets standards relating to the cleanliness of the outlet and the grooming of employees.

The federal definition of a franchise includes the following qualification:

> *"The franchisor exerts or has the authority to exert a significant degree of control over the franchisee's method of operation, including but not limited to, the franchisee's business organization, promotional activities, management, marketing plan or business affairs; or (2) the*

franchisor gives significant assistance to the franchisee in the latter's method of operation..."

Thus, a franchise must also involve "a significant degree of control" and "significant assistance" by the franchisor. A franchisor may exert control by setting mandatory procedures, product specifications, and so forth. A franchisor may provide assistance in the form of a training program, an operating manual, and ongoing help with advertising, inventory planning, and purchasing.

The more a franchisee relies upon the franchisor's control or assistance, the more likely the control or assistance will be considered "significant." In addition, to be deemed significant under federal regulations, the control or assistance must relate to the overall business operation, not just a small aspect.

Significant types of control or assistance include:

- Site selection or approval
- Outlet design or appearance standards
- Stipulated business hours
- Mandated production techniques
- Specified accounting practices
- Mandatory personnel policies
- Co-op advertising
- Territorial restrictions
- Formal training
- Management, marketing, or hiring advice
- Provision of a website
- Franchise operating manual

To a lesser extent, inventory controls, display standards, and assistance with sales or repairs may also fall under the FTC's "Significant Control or Assistance Element."

Some activities that are not considered "significant" under the Rule include advertising displays, product samples, trademark controls, and health or safety restriction already mandated by federal or state laws.

The Required Payment Element

The third component of a franchise under the FTC definition is a financial consideration, explained as follows:

> "The franchisee is required as a condition of obtaining or commencing the franchise operation to make a payment or a commitment to pay to the franchisor, or to a person affiliated with the franchisor.."

A payment by a franchisee does not have to be labeled a franchise fee to satisfy this element of the definition. Ongoing royalty payments or payments characterized otherwise, such as consulting fees, training fees, or site assistance fees, are sufficient, as long as they are for the right to operate the business.

The "Required Payment Element" kicks in if the purchaser is required to pay to the franchisor, or any affiliate, $500 or more, within the first six months of the opening of the business. This condition embraces all sources of revenue that a franchisee is required to pay to the franchisor, including the following:

- Initial franchise fee
- Lease or rent
- Advertising costs
- Purchase of equipment and supplies
- Training fees
- Security deposits
- Bookkeeping charges;
- Purchase of promotional literature
- Equipment rental
- Continuing royalties on sales

It should be noted that purchasing "reasonable amounts of inventory at bona fide wholesale prices" is not considered a required payment under the Amended Franchise Rule.

Simply stated, any business relationship or opportunity is legally a franchise if it includes a trademark license, quality standards, management controls, operating assistance, and one or more payments.

Exemptions to the Rules

Both federal and state rules and laws exempt certain types of business relationships and enterprises from the franchise regulations. At the federal level, these exceptions include employer-employee relationships, general partnerships, cooperative associations, and departments within a department store.

In addition, a franchise that accounts for no more than 20% of the gross sales of the franchise holder are also exempt from FTC rules. This type of franchise is called a "fractional" franchise. For example, a franchise to sell flavored ice within a convenience store would be exempted if the receipts were no more than 20% of the store's total revenues.

Different exemptions are granted by various states. For example, California law exempts gasoline service stations and bank credit card services.

Operational Anatomy

From an operational perspective, a modern business format franchise has the following basic components:

1. A licensed identity, usually including a trade name and logo.
2. An operating system or business format, consisting of specifications, quality standards, and prescribed

products or methods of operation.
3. A support system, usually consisting of training and ongoing assistance with marketing, advertising, purchasing, and other operational aspects of the business.
4. A continuous financial relationship, usually a lump sum paid in advance, plus an ongoing royalty based on an established percentage of gross revenues.

The identity and business format, in most cases, are owned by the franchisor or an entity with which the franchisor has contracted. In some cases, a franchise opportunity may be based on marketing rights to an exclusive product, rather than a business format. The franchisee is an independent business owner who contracts with the franchisor to obtain the right to put these components to use. The franchisee provides the working capital to establish and develop the outlet. In many franchise opportunities, the difference between success or failure lies in the ongoing services provided to franchisees.

The International Franchise Association defines a franchise using promotional verbiage, as follows:

"A franchise is a continuing relationship between franchisor and franchisee in which the sum total of the franchisor's knowledge, image, success, manufacturing, and marketing techniques are supplied to the franchisee for a consideration."

The franchisee pays a financial consideration to the franchisor and invests the money required to start the business. The franchisor supplies an optimized business system or exclusive product, a recognizable identity, and know-how. The franchisee must usually abide by the franchisor's quality standards and product specifications. Yet, despite this relationship, a franchisor and a franchisee are not legal business partners. The franchisee is the exclusive owner of the business.

In many cases, purchasing a franchise means acquiring a pre-packaged business. However, although the franchisee owns all the assets, the franchisor may have a strong voice in how the business is run. The cornerstone of every franchise is a contract that defines the rights and obligations of the franchisor and the franchisee.

From an operational perspective, a business format franchise elaborates on the federal and state legal definition. Whereas the legal perspective focuses on what does—and does not—constitute a franchise under regulations and laws, the operational perspective focuses on the aspects of a franchise relationship that form the basis of the business arrangement and contribute to the likelihood of success. The following are typical components:

1. Licensed Trademark

The franchisee receives the right to use the franchisor's trademark, name, logo, or other commercial symbol, thus taking advantage of the parent company's reputation and image. For example, a franchisee licensed to use the McDonald's trademark benefits from major national television advertising and the image of an industry giant.

2. Training Program

The franchisee receives training in operating the franchise business, usually at the franchisor's headquarters or at a designed site. Industry-wide, franchise training programs range from two days to six months. A typical curriculum consists of the following subjects: industry background; outlet development; accounting, purchasing and inventory methods; product preparation, manufacturing, or merchanising; sales and marketing; advertising and promotion; staff hiring and training. Additional technical or industry-specific training may also be offered, depending on the business and the franchise.

Refresher courses, periodic seminars, and annual confernces may also be offered by the franchisor.

3. Operations Manual

The franchisor's trade secrets, know-how, and experience are usually documented in a confidential operations manual loaned to franchisees for the term of the franchise. A good manual includes detailed policies, procedures, and techniques for starting and developing the outlet, ordering initial supplies and inventory, pricing and merchandising, preparing or selling products, outlet management, hiring and training staff, personnel policies, bookkeeping techniques, and technical aspects of the business.

Many franchise operations manuals are divided into series, with separate volumes devoted to daily operating procedures, management policies, marketing and adverising, technical operations, and so forth.

4. Specifications, Blueprints, and Designs

Franchisors often provide specifications and designs for building and operating the outlet. Examples include architectural plans, construction blueprints, and designs for fixtures and signs. Franchisors may also provide approved supplier lists, suggested or mandatory opening inventory lists, and detailed specifications for equipment and ingredients, where applicable.

Food service franchisors commonly provide franchisees with secret recipes or ingredients, such as premade dough for bakery goods or patented syrups for bottled soft drinks.

5. Advertising Systems

More than half of franchisors administer or provide for a cooperative advertising fund, to which franchisees contribute a small percentage of their outlets' gross revenues. This pool is generally used to finance major national or regional campaigns to the benefit of all franchisees.

Franchisors may also assist individual outlet owners through the preparation of standard advertising materials, such as fliers, commercials, or camera-ready artwork for newspaper or magazine advertisements. Most franchise agreements force franchisees to abide by their franchisors' advertising standards and to use only artwork and language approved by the franchisor's advertising department.

6. Ongoing Assistance

A typical business format franchise includes provisions for ongoing assistance, such as on-site troubleshooting and guidance by a field manager or consultant. Franchisees may also have access to company advisers via a toll-free "hotline."

As franchisors improve their business systems and operating methods, they invariably share innovations with their franchisees or upgrade the image of their outlets.

7. A Valued Identity

Foremost, a franchisor offers its good name in the industry. A successful identity is one of the hallmarks of a franchise offering. Therefore, the franchisor must be capable of substantiating its value. Much of the value of a franchise identity is derived from the recognition, reputation, and goodwill of the franchise organization. People buy products from vendors that are familiar to them.

Likewise, people who invest in franchises are looking for a successful image. Anyone who takes on a franchise, takes on the franchisor's identity.

Trademarks are protected on both federal and local levels. Federal protection is secured by registering a trademark with the Registrar of Patents and Trademarks. Before a trademark is registered at the federal level, a search is first conducted to ascertain whether the same trademark has been previously registered by another party.

If no prior registration is found, the trademark receives "applied for" status, permitting the applicant to use the symbol "TM" in association with the trademark. A one-year waiting period, in which the trademark may be contested by others, is required before the trademark is officially "registered," and the owner may use the (R) symbol in conjunction with the trademark.

Trademarks are often registered at the state or county level, as well. In disputes over trademark rights, the earliest registration, whether local or federal, generally applies in a particular locality. For example, even though a trademark may be registered at the federal level, another party who obtained a local registration for the same trademark on an earlier date may be entitled to trademark in his or her locality.

A section of the Franchise Disclosure Document (FDD) is devoted to trademarks and trade names. In Section 13 of that document, franchisors are required to describe "any trademark, service mark, trade name, logotype or other commercial symbols to be licensed to the franchisee." Each mark, name, logo, or symbol which the franchisee will be entitled to use must be identified. In addition, the franchisor must state whether any of the trademarks and service marks have been registered with the United States Patent and Trademark Office, or whether an application for registration is pending.

A license to use a trademark or trade name does not, by itself, constitute a franchise, but a trademark license is an integral element of any franchise relationship. The name must be exclusive, but it may apply either to the products distributed by the franchisee or to the business itself.
Control and Assistance

Typically, the types of control and assistance exerted by a franchisor include an exclusive territory, training in the operation of the business, site selection or approval, streamlined production or selling techniques, personnel policies, assistance with advertising and promotion, and quality standards. Such controls or assistance are often referred to as "a community of interest" between the franchisor and franchisee.

The franchise agreement, the formal contract between the franchisor and the franchisee, spells out the rights and obligations of both parties. For example, the franchise agreement may obligate the franchisor to provide a training program, and restrict the franchisee from owning another business that competes directly with the franchise outlet.

The franchisor's advice, specifications, and quality standards may be contained in publication called, fittingly, the franchise operating manual. Among other subjects, a typical operating manual covers bookkeeping practices, maintenance procedures, sales techniques, advertising policies, personnel hiring and training, inventory control, and purchasing.

The franchise operating manual is the franchisor's "bible." It documents the business format and sets forth the standards and policies that all franchisees are expected to follow.

One of the most important considerations of a franchise opportunity is the ease with which the business format can be transferred to the franchisee. Some one who buys a franchise expects to acquire more than just a trademark, but also a finely-tuned business system.

Some franchisors go so far as to provide a complete "turnkey" business: when the franchisee graduates from the franchisor's training school, he or she receives a fully developed outlet. However, it is more common for a franchisor to provide blueprints, manuals, specifications, and training, relying on the franchisee's initiative to get the business established.

The franchisor usually loans the operating manual to the franchisee for the term of the franchise agreement. On expiration or termination of the franchise, the book must be returned to the franchisor. This requirement helps to protect the franchisor's trade secrets and maintain the aura of secrecy about the business system. After all, if the formula wasn't secret, why would you pay good money to obtain it?

Fees and Payments

In return for the franchisor's valued identity and finely tuned operating system, a business format franchisee pays a fee. Typically, franchise fees are of three types:

- An initial fee, due on signing the franchise agreement
- An ongoing royalty charged on the gross revenues of the outlet
- Other royalties or fees for advertising, consultation, or other assistance

A new franchise opportunity or a franchise offered by a small chain may charge a relatively low initial fee. Conversely, the larger the chain, the more you can expect to pay for the privilege of joining. For example, the first Burger King franchises sold for as little as $300, and the first McDonald's franchisee paid an initial fee of just $1,000. Today, a franchisee might pay as much as $30,000 for either of these franchises.

Why is an established franchise more valuable than a new one? For one thing, an experienced franchisor has a demonstrated track record. For another, the sheer number of outlets maximizes such collective benefits as co-op advertising and volume purchasing.

Note that, in the FTC definition, a business relationship is not a franchise unless a financial consideration is paid by the franchisee. Specifically, the total payment or obligation during the first six months of the franchisee's operation must be more than $500. If this condition is not met, the arrangement is not a true franchise under FTC requirements and, thus, might be exempt from at least a portion of the federal rules.

The Strategic Perspective

Ultimately, a successful franchise outcome depends on the motivational and financial qualifications of the outlet's owner/operators. However, in recent years, strategic investment in franchises has become increasingly important to the economic health of storefront-based businesses. The strategic perspective is based on evaluation of the following:

- Return on Investment (ROI)
- Multi-unit performance
- Growth potential of the brand
- Resale profitability
- Stock market performance (where applicable)

Investors view Return on Investment (ROI) in two different ways: (1) the ratio of net profits to total assets, and (2) the length of time it takes a business to return to investors the monies they invested in the enterprise. The first method simply requires dividing net profits by total assets. For example, if the net profits of the business are $300,000 and the total assets of the business equal $500,000, the ratio of profits-to-assets is 60%. Another way to conceptualize the ROI for a new business is the point at which investors realize a return on their investment. This point requires estimating when the business will begin to realize sufficient profits to repay the original amount invested.

In recent years, multi-unit franchise ownership by passive or semi-passive investors has become increasingly common. The growth potential of a franchise brand must be weighed against the initial investment. The buying and reselling of franchise outlets currently accounts for nearly 50% of all turnover in the industry. Single-unit and multi-unit owners alike are concerned with resale profitability.

Franchising companies that are publicly traded on the stock market are vulnerable to numerous influences. The most resilient have managed to endure despite market fluctuations and unanticipated cycles in the buying and selling of stocks.

When the stock market was created, stocks represented an ownership share in the company that issued them. Over time, stock prices were deemed by investors to represent the overall worth of the issuing entity, taking into account its assets, cash flow, and financial position. Early trading strategies were based on the analysis of the potential value of a company's stock in relation to its offering price.

Since the 1990s, actual worth has declined in importance in relation to human sentiment, expressed as the reaction to current events, personal opinions, and intuition about the future. Driven by price manipulation, with little or no relation to the actual worth of the issuing company, today's stock markets are often compared to casino gambling and lotteries.

In the current investing environment, human emotions are disproportionately influential, especially when negative events occur. An airplane crash can send airline stocks on a downward spiral, a terrorist attack on a hotel can doom hotel stocks, or a celebrity's choice of clothing at a red carpet event can make or break the stocks of apparel companies.

Franchise Semantics

When is a franchise not a franchise? Conversely, when is a so-called "business opportunity," "distributorship," or "dealership" really a franchise offering? In some cases, investments that are promoted as franchises do not have all the essential components. The term franchise implies backing, support, and a strong likelihood of success. Yet many so-called franchise offerings are little more than trade name licenses or highly priced sales territories. Do these types of offerings fall under franchise regulation?

Some states, such as California, consider an investment offering to be a franchise whenever the word "franchise" is used in promotion. But what about the carefully named "business opportunity" that seems to have the components of a franchise but is promoted as a completely different type of investment?

A franchise does not have to be called a franchise to come within the scope of state laws or federal regulations. In fact, franchise regulators in some states spend the greater part of their time investigating franchise-like opportunities in order to identify unethical operators attempting to skirt the law.

In most states that regulate franchise sales, any business that sells the right to a trade name or business format and received a payment for that right is a franchise, no matter what term the promoter may use to describe the investment. Be wary of any promoter who claims not to be a franchisor but offers you the right to use a trade name for a fee.

One should be wary, as well, of the self-styled "franchisor" who fails to provide all the ingredients of success: a recognizable trademark, a tested business format, training, promotional assistance, specifications, blueprints, designs, ongoing guidance, and a proven track record of success.

5
THE ECONOMICS OF FRANCHISING

"Details create the big picture."
Sanford I. Weill

Depending on one's perspective or financial capability, a franchise investment can seem relatively small or exorbitant. The cost of admission is not necessarily related to the return on investment. At the low end are home-based or mobile businesses requiring $10,000 or less. At the high end are hotel franchises costing $5 million or more. A typical fast-food outlet costs $250,000 to $1 million or more to open, whereas a full-service restaurant may require an investment of $600,000 to $3 million.

Franchise fees generally run between $20,000 to $30,000, but can top $100,000 for high-end brands. Once the business is up and running, there are ongoing royalties to pay, ranging from four percent to eight percent of gross revenues. An ongoing assessment for cooperative advertising is also usually part of the deal.

In addition to the franchise fees and startup costs, a franchise buyer occurs legal and accounting costs to evaluate and close the deal, averaging $3,000 to $12,000 or more.

Franchisors usually have minimum financial requirements based on the applicant's net worth and total liquid assets. For example, a Burger King franchise has an initial investment of about $2.2 million, requiring a minimum of $1.5 million in net worth and $500,000 in liquid assets.

In recent years, some franchisors have begun offering discounts to veterans, minorities, and women. Such incentives include lower initial franchise fees and/or reduced royalty payments. Responding to downtrends in the economy, many franchisors occasionally offer limited promotional incentives, such as discounted franchise fees and royalties, deferred payments, and money-back guarantees.

Almost any type of financial consideration that a franchise buyer is required to pay to a franchisor, or an affiliate of the franchisor, is considered a franchise fee, including charges for training, advertising, deposits, signs, or royalties. A typical business format franchise has three basic financial components: the initial fee, the franchise royalty, and an advertising royalty.

Beyond these, a franchisor may sell fixtures, equipment, specially outfitted vehicles, signs, or promotional materials— all of which also constitute a fee under the FTC's Amended Franchise Rule. Requiring a franchisee to purchase inventory from the franchisor or its affiliate may be excluded, if the cost is in line with other sources. Charges for training, site selection, or other guidance are specifically defined as franchise fees by the FTC Rule.

Virtually every franchise offering includes an initial fee.

The Initial Fee

In all but a few cases, upon signing the franchise agreement, the franchisee is required to pay an initial fee. However, an advance deposit may be required as a means of proving the buyer's serious intent to follow through with the purchase. The fee amount set by the franchisor should have a quantifiable and verifiable basis. In theory, the initial fee compensates the franchisor for the costs of putting the franchisee in business. Typically, the fee is applied by the franchisor toward such costs as recruiting and training the franchisee, and assisting with business planning and start-up.

Various state laws require the cost components of the initial fee to be itemized, so as to minimize the amount of "blue sky," or unjustifiable costs, included in the total. In addition, the Securities Exchange Commission prohibits corporations that sell franchises from including initial fees as income until the fees "are fully earned" by the franchisor. In other words, the franchisor must fulfill all its obligations to the franchisee before the money can be counted as income.

Initial fees charged by franchisors range from $10,000 to $30,000 to a hundred thousand or more. The average initial fee is $17,800.

A franchisor's initial fees may take into consideration the following factors:

1. the value of the business, including its goodwill
2. the value of the market or territory
3. the average cost of recruiting a franchisee
4. the average cost of training a franchisee
5. the cost of signs, ads, plans, or other aids

In some cases, the franchisee may not be required to pay a franchise fee, but, instead, to purchase supplies or equipment from the franchisor or a designated supplier. Even so, under federal regulations, such a payment is considered to constitute an initial franchise fee. In this type of arrangement, none of the above factors are in play, and the franchise should be regarded as high-risk.

The Value of the Business

"Goodwill" refers to the reputation of the business and its ability to attract new or repeat customers. As such, goodwill is considered an asset of a business, because when the business is sold, its goodwill will be transferred to the new owner.

However, in franchising, the value of goodwill is often perceived, not calculated. Thus, it nearly always equals demand. In other words, goodwill is never less valuable than the maximum amount anyone is willing to pay for it. For instance, how much more valuable is the right to own a restaurant named McDonald's than the right to own one named Fuddrucker's? The answer is: whatever someone is willing to pay.

When a company first begins offering franchises for sale, it has no franchises sold or open, though it may have one or even scores of company-owned outlets. Even so, the initial fee should have a tangible basis beyond mere guesswork.

In most franchise offerings, at least part of the initial fee represents the value of goodwill. Though such a value may seem elusive or hypothetical, there are some ways to place a fair price on goodwill. An investment broker often estimates goodwill at four to twelve percent of the market value of the business. The market value is estimated by multiplying annual profits times 2.5.

For example, if a business generates $30,000 per year in net profits, the market value may be calculated as follows:

$$300,000 \times 2.5 = 750,000$$

In this example, the business should theoretically be worth about $750,000. Figured at four percent, the value of goodwill would be calculated as follows:

$$750,000 \times .04 = 30,000$$

In this instance, the value of goodwill is about $30,000. At 12%—an exceptionally high rate—the value would be $75,000.

The value of a brand new franchise with fewer than ten outlets is essentially hypothetical. Hence, demand almost always dictates the value. Based on the maximum price the seller can command, the same franchise may sell for different prices at different times or in different parts of the country. Bear in mind that in the case of an established franchise, the seller may not be the franchisor, but rather a franchise broker, an area developer, or an existing franchise owners reselling his outlet.

As a general rule, the more outlets, the higher the initial fee. For example, a franchisor might start out offering franchises at an initial fee of only a few hundred dollars. In some instances, some franchises might be granted without charging any initial fee, simply to build momentum.

If you are considering a franchise that is just getting off the ground, a "sweetheart" deal is not out of the question. No matter how successful the franchisor's original business, if the company does not yet have a track record in franchising, the initial fee should be considered negotiable. If you invest in such a franchise, you will be assume a proportionately higher risk and are justified in expecting some form of compensation or compromise.

The Value of the Market

Besides the intangible value of the business identity and goodwill, the initial fee should also reflect the value of an exclusive territory or trading area. In this case, the franchisor may base part of the fee on population statistics, demographics, or sales surveys to estimate the relative worth of a specific territory. For example, some real estate franchises charge a set amount for each 100,000 people in the territory.

The franchisor may carve out franchise territories of equal value, or vary the initial fee based on the relative worth of the market.

The value of the market is determined by the type of territory the franchisee receives and the potential sales of the franchise product or service within than territory. The franchisor should have a detailed and consistent method of identifying and defining territories. Some territories may be defined simply by zip code, while others may be based on demographic content.

An exclusive territory is one in which the franchisor agrees not open another outlet in competition with the franchisee's outlet. The territory may be static—that is, it may remain the same throughout the duration of the franchise agreement—or it may be subject to revision based on the franchisee's sales performance. For example, if a certain sales level is attained, the franchisee may have the right to expand the territory. Conversely, if sales fall below a certain level, the franchisor may have the right to reduce the territory.

The size of the territory may range from a city block to an entire country. However, courts have ruled that franchisees may not be prohibited from selling to customers outside an exclusive territory. In fact, in urban areas, relatively small territories may be located in close proximity to one another, resulting in franchisees selling to customers in neighboring territories.

Potential sales are often calculated on the basis of similar units operating in comparable markets. Sales and marketing data are also be used to establish the value of a proposed territory. The relative value of territories is established from analytics. For example, according to statistical analysis, the value of a territory for a franchise engaged in retail sales in Los Angeles is 8.5 times higher than one in Phoenix. One might expect, therefore, that a territory in Phoenix would be priced proportionately lower, for a comparable market size with similar demographics. For analytical purposes, each region of the United States is divided into Sales and Marketing Statistical Areas (SMSAs), for which sales of various products and services are gathered annually. To compensate for the discrepancy in the value of geographic territories, franchisors often adjust the size of the territory based on SMSA data and demographics, so that the initial fee remains the same for every franchisee.

The Cost of Putting the Franchisee in Business

The remaining components of an initial fee, mainly, the costs that are attributable to putting the franchisee in business, are more tangible. For example, the average cost of recruiting a franchisee can be estimated with a fair degree of accuracy. This amount might include costs attributable to advertising, lead processing, administration, and accounting. Similarly, the franchisee training program has an identifiable cost that must be integrated into the initial fee. In addition, the franchisor may need to recover the costs of printing the franchise operating manual, preparing architectural plans, and assisting with site selection, signs, and other activities.

As an example, assume a franchising company plans to sell 100 franchises in the forthcoming fiscal year. If the company's annual advertising budget is $120,000, it will cost an average of $1,200 to recruit each franchisee. Let's say the company's annual operating budget includes $250,000 to run the franchisee training school. Thus, the average training cost will run $2,500 per franchisee. This hypothetical franchisor must already charge at least $3,700 per franchise just to cover its costs. Add to that figure such costs as the franchise operating manual, site selection assistance, communications, etc., and it is not difficult to see why initial fees of $15,000 to $30,000 are common.

The following is an example of such a valuation:

Average advertising cost per franchisee	$1,200
Average training cost per franchisee	$2,500
Average administrative cost per franchisee	$3,600
Architectural plans and blueprints	$2,500

Franchise operating manual	$500
Site selection and grand opening costs	$2,500
Value of market	$7,200
Goodwill	$5,000
Total initial fee	$25,000

As the example illustrates, the initial fee is designed to compensate the franchisor for the cost of putting the franchisee in business. There is no built-in profit margin. The only "blue sky" is the value of goodwill, which can often be verified by analyzing the sales of comparable outlets.

If a franchisor has relatively few outlets, you would be justified in expecting the initial fee to be proportionately low—just enough to cover recruiting, training, and administrative costs. Buying a franchise from an established franchising company that has a well-known brand, you would expect a disproportionately high value to be placed on goodwill and intangibles.

Ongoing Franchise Fees

Besides an initial fee, most franchise investments also involve an ongoing payment for the duration of the franchise agreement. Typically, a royalty is charged on the gross sales or net revenues of the franchisee's outlet. Gross sales are the total receipts before expenses are deducted. Net revenues are total sales after deducting expenses. Needless to say, the difference is significant.

To illustrate, assume a business realizes $500,000 in gross sales before deducting expenses. If the franchise royalty is 5%, the franchisee pays $25,000 to the franchisor. However, if, for example, the expenses of the business are $375,000, the net revenues would $125,000 and the royalty payment, based on 5%, would be $6,250.

Franchise royalties range from one half of one to fifteen percent of gross sales. The average franchise royalty is five percent of gross sales. A typical franchise agreement defines gross sales as "the actual receipts of the outlet, after deducting any refunds, returns, and taxes collected." In other words, royalties are not charged for sales tax paid by customers or for purchases that are refunded or returned.

The percentage of franchisors that base the franchise royalty on net sales is relatively small.

In lieu of a royalty, a fixed fee may be payable at weekly or monthly intervals. In some cases, the ongoing fee is hidden in the franchisor's markup of goods or supplies that the franchisor sells to franchisees.

A franchise royalty, like the initial fee, should reflect both the worth and maturity of the organization. The first franchises sold by a franchisor are often offered at a relatively low royalty. As more outlets begin to open, the initial fee and royalty may be increased. To illustrate, assume a franchisor first sets the initial fee at $10,000 and the monthly royalty at 3.5 percent of gross sales to attract franchisees. At this appealing price, the franchisor rapidly sells six franchises, thereby increasing the actual and perceived value of the business. The franchisor is now justified in hiking the initial fee to $15,000, and the monthly royalty to five percent.

However, that by itself does not mean that the existing six franchisees have to pay more than the original royalty for which they signed up. Numerous court cases have established that a franchisor cannot raise the royalty fee paid by franchisees already under contract. The franchisor is obliged to honor their franchise agreements as long as the franchisee is in business. However, the new fees can be levied on any subsequent, as-yet-unsold franchisees.

Both the initial fee and the royalty are required to be disclosed in the franchisor's offering circular, so any increase requires a new disclosure document as well as an amendment to the application for franchise registration in such states as California, Illinois, New York, and 13 others.

Assume our hypothetical franchisor sells another twelve franchises at the higher price. The value of the franchise has increased still more, so the franchisor raises the initial fee to $15,000, and the royalty to 7.5 percent. The franchisor now has six franchisees who paid $10,000 each in initial fees and continue to pay a royalty of 3.5 percent of gross monthly revenues. In addition, another twelve who paid $15,000 in initial fees are paying out five percent of their gross incomes. But anyone else who buys a franchise from Golden Opportunities will have to pay the new amount—$20,000 plus 7.5 percent.

Higher initial fees and royalties generally indicate a more mature organization. When franchise opportunities are evaluated, a franchisor's fees should be compared with others in the same field, by contrasting the size, experience, and recognition of the franchise chain with the others. The following questions are pertinent:

Are the fees justifiable in relation to competition?

Do they accurately reflect the franchisor's number of years in the industry?

Does the franchisor have more outlets than franchisors that command lower fees?

Royalties vary significantly from one franchise to another. A car rental franchisee may pay 7.5 percent of gross monthly sales to the franchisor, whereas a hotel franchisee may pay five percent, or the owner of an ice cream parlor just one-half to one percent. Besides a franchise royalty, many franchisors also derive profits from the sale or lease of products, supplies, or equipment to franchisees. Thus, although a royalty may seem low superficially, the total cash outlay to the franchisor, in fact, is usually substantial.

Advertising Fees

An advertising fee is a separate payment above and beyond the ongoing royalty, earmarked for promotional assistance. Typically, advertising fees may be accrued in a joint national or regional fund, to finance major promotional campaigns on behalf of all the contributing franchisees. The most common type of advertising fee is a royalty on the gross sales of the franchisee's outlet. In some cases, a set fee is assessed for promotional assistance.

Typically, advertising fees are paid into a co-op fund. Monies accruing in this fund are pooled to finance national and regional advertising campaigns for the benefit of all franchisees.

A co-op ad fund benefits an individual franchise owner by financing major advertising programs that would be otherwise unaffordable. The franchisor benefits from increased exposure of the trade name and business, thus increasing the value of both its product and franchise.

Note that not all franchisors maintain a co-op ad fund. Many franchise systems require franchisees to conduct and pay for their own promotions. Unhappily, this practice sometimes leads to a loss of control over the business image. It also tends to alienate franchisees if advertising standards deteriorate. After all, it is the security of sameness that attracts consumers to franchise establishments in the first place.

Advertising royalties are not always placed in a co-op fund. In some cases, the money ends up in the general operating fund of the franchise corporation. More than one franchise agreement empowers the franchisor to spend franchisees' advertising royalties any way the franchisor chooses. For a franchisee, that's not necessarily a bad arrangement. Often, a franchisor does not know the most effective way to promote its outlets. Still, when evaluating a franchise opportunity, it is worth investigating where advertising fees go and who controls how they are spent. Some advertising funds are controlled by a committee of franchisees.

Advertising royalties range from a fraction of one percent to several percentage points. As of this writing, Haagen Dazs franchisees pay ten cents per gallon of ice cream sold, whereas Travelodge franchisees pay four percent of room sales. Manhattan Bagel franchisees pay one half of one percent of their gross revenues. One franchisor in the building construction field charges $100 per month for advertising.

Like franchise royalties, advertising royalties may be subject to periodic increases, which cannot be unilaterally levied on existing franchise outlets. However, in theory a cooperative ad fund benefits all outlets equally, and so charging different franchisees different rates might be viewed as a dubious practice.

There is a tendency, when investigating a franchise opportunity, to focus on franchise fees and royalties, overlooking a much more meaningful price component: the total initial investment.

The Initial Investment

On the surface, a franchise with an initial fee of $10,000 might seem like a bargain compared to one offered for $35,000. But a more meaningful comparison is to contrast the total initial investments. How much will it cost to start the business? What is the cost of equipment, supplies, and inventory? How much money will be required to sustain the business until it begins to return a profit?

The Franchisor Disclosure Document (FDD), which by law every franchisor is required to provide to a prospective franchisee, must include a breakdown of the initial investment. A typical breakdown shows the initial fee plus the cost of procuring and developing a site. It must also show the cost of all equipment, leases, fixtures, and inventory required to operate the business.

It may also include working capital for out-of-pocket expenses before the business becomes profitable. Franchisors are not obligated to follow a specific formula for estimating working capital requirements.

Many factors affect the total initial investment, including the location, industry, local wage scale, and state of the economy. Franchisors often provide high and low estimates for the same type of outlet, realizing that it might cost fifty percent more to develop a business in San Francisco, California than to develop one Greensboro, North Carolina.

The following chart shows the initial investment breakdown for a typical retail outlet.

Item	How paid	Amount	When due	Paid to
Initial Fee	Lump sum	$25,000	Signing	Franchisor
Equipment	As ordered	$27,000	As ordered	Vendors
Lease deposit	As agreed	$3,600	As agreed	Lessor
Improvements	As agreed	$9,000	As ordered	Vendors
Inventory	As ordered	$35,000	As ordered	Suppliers
Licenses/permits	---	$1,000	As agreed	Various
Insurance	As ordered	$1,800	As agreed	Carrier
Working capital	---	$9,000	---	Various
Total		$111,400		

Franchise Organization and Fees

Franchise fees may be influenced by the way in which the franchise system is organized. If a franchise is obtained from a subfranchisor, the outlet's royalty payments may be shared by both the subfranchisor and the original franchisor. A subfranchisor, or master franchisee, has the rights to sell franchises within a specified territory, under a master franchise agreement with the franchisor.

The organization of a franchise system is called the ultrastructure. A satellite system is the simplest form of ultrastructure. Like moons revolving around a planet, each franchise is an independent satellite operating under the global influence of the franchisor. In this type of organization, each outlet is directly accountable to the franchisor. There are no subfranchisors or other marketing levels between the franchisor and the franchisee. Likewise, the initial fee and franchise royalties are paid directly to the franchisor by each franchisee.

If you a franchise is obtained in a satellite system, the franchisee may also obtain an exclusive territory in which the franchisor promises not to sell another franchise outlet. Some states have laws requiring franchisors operating in those jurisdictions to protect the marketing territories of franchises.

By granting a territory and agreeing not compete with you within that territory, a franchisor creates value for the franchise. What is a franchise territory worth? The answer to that question depends, among other things, on the nature of the business, the size of the territory, and local economic conditions.

Evaluating a Franchise Territory

A shrewd franchisor knows only too well that each geographical area, or portion thereof, has a different value as a franchise territory. For example, retail sales in Los Angeles, California are about ten times higher than those in Providence, Rhode Island. If a franchisor grants an exclusive territory, the boundaries may be based on such factors as population, demographics, or sales. A typical franchise territory may be as large as a country or as small as a city block.

Area Franchising

Large market areas are sometimes granted in association with master franchises or area franchises. In this strategy, the franchisor licenses to a "master" or area franchisee subfranchising rights to a large territory—for example, a state, a region consisting of multiple states, or an entire country. The area franchisor receives the right to sell satellite franchises in the territory. The master franchise agreement may restrict the number of subfranchises that can be sold. However, in some cases, the master franchisee is free to establish as many outlets as he can sell.

Area franchising is commonly used in the real estate industry. For, the Century 21 Real Estate system was built on this concept. A master franchisee who purchased area rights to a large geographical territory received the right to subfranchise many Century 21 offices. The individual outlets function as satellites of the master franchise. The franchisor, in turn, controls the master franchisees. Each satellite pays initial fees and royalties to the area franchisor, who then pays royalties to the franchisor.

To maintain control over the various levels and sublevels of the franchise system, the franchisor has a team of "area controllers." But the master franchisee shoulders the burden of recruiting and, in some cases, training franchisees.

By area franchising, a franchisor maximizes short-term cash flow while minimizing overhead. Consider a franchisor planning to sell 300 franchises in one year. The recruiting and administrative costs alone would be staggering. However, instead of selling and supporting individual outlets, the company might opt to sell off subfranchising rights to several large regions.

Let's say this franchisor finds a master franchisee willing to pay $100,000 for subfranchising rights in one of the regions. With one transaction, the franchisor may realize as much income as he would have by selling ten individual outlets. Yet, the company would also avoid the costs of recruiting, training, and putting the franchisees in business. In this way, the franchisor sacrifices a share of the long-term cash flow to produce a higher short-term income.

Trade Name Franchising

Another hybrid form of franchising is the trade name franchise. In a trade name franchise, the franchisor licenses a franchisee to use a particular name or trademark in conjunction with the distribution of a particular product or service. Coca-Cola, Pepsi-Cola, and Seven-Up are probably the most recognizable trade-name franchises. Bottlers buy the right to use the soft-drink trademark and obtain access to the recipe or syrup from which the product is made. But they do not receive a comprehensive business format. In fact, a typical soft drink bottler may have contracts with more than one franchisor. Thus, in some markets, the same company that has the Coca-Cola franchise might also bottle Dr. Pepper and Orange Crush.

Obviously, a trade name franchise must have a well-recognized brand name or trademark to justify its value.

Evaluating Franchise Fees and Payments

When a franchise opportunity is evaluated, it is important to determine exactly what type of franchise being offered, as well as what type is best for the investor.

Do you need training? Is a prepackaged business format important, or is a famous trademark enough? Do you want direct access to the franchisor, or would you be content dealing with a subfranchisor or master franchisee?

6
FULL AND ACCURATE DISCLOSURE

"Truth is a thing immortal and eternal; it gives us not a beauty that fades with time, nor does it take away the confident speech that is based on justice, but confirms things just and lawful, distinguishing things unjust from them and showing their falsehood."
                                                            Epictetus

A rising tide of scandals, ranging from disgruntled franchise buyers to outright frauds, prompted various states to enact laws protecting investors against potential abuses by unscrupulous franchisors. Eventually, the federal government also entered the regulatory picture.

This chapter looks at federal and state regulations governing the registration, offer, and sale of franchises, from advertising and recruitment, to initial contact and "full and accurate disclosure."

Federal Franchise Regulations

At the federal level, the offer and sale of franchise opportunities fall under the jurisdiction of the Federal Trade Commission (FTC). The FTC was created by the Federal Trade Commission Act, which became law on September 26, 1914. The commission effectively replaced the federal Bureau of Corporations, which had previously been responsible for overseeing business practices in the United States. Since its conception, the primary mission of the FTC has been to prevent monopolies and preserve competition in commerce.

President Woodrow Wilson hailed the Act as an important safeguard of the free enterprise system, a means "to make men in a small way of business as free to succeed as men in a big way" and to "kill monopoly in the seed."

Section Five of the Act begins:

> *Unfair methods of competition in commerce, and unfair or deceptive acts or practices in commerce, are declared unlawful.*

The FTC has the power to make regulations and issue rules that have the full impact and enforcement of federal law. The Commission is further empowered to bring legal proceedings against any person or company that transgresses a regulation or rule

On December 21, 1978, the Commission drafted an amendment to Title 16 of the Code of Federal Regulations, which deals with Commerce and Trade. The amendment was aimed at regulating the sale of franchises and business opportunity ventures. The new rules went into effect on October 21, 1979, requiring franchisors to disclose certain pertinent information to prospective franchisees before any sale is made. The franchise rule also affected the manner in which franchisors may make any claims regarding actual or potential sales or earnings of a prospective franchisee.

A sweeping amended rule began to be phased in during 2007, eventually replacing the original franchise rule in its entirety, effective July 1, 2008.

The definitions and requirements of the Amended Franchise Rule are found in Part 436 of the Code of Federal Regulations. Section 436.2 begins as follows:

> *"In connection with the offer or sale of a franchise to be located in the United States of America or its territories, unless the transaction is exempted under subpart E of this*

part, it is an unfair or deceptive act or practice in violation of Section 5 of the Federal Trade Commission Act:

(a) For any franchisor to fail to furnish a prospective franchisee with a copy of the franchisor's current disclosure document, as described in subparts C and D of this part, at least 14 calendar-days before the prospective franchisee signs a binding agreement with, or makes any payment to, the franchisor or an affiliate in connection with the proposed franchise sale.

(b) For any franchisor to alter unilaterally and materially the terms and conditions of the basic franchise agreement or any related agreements attached to the disclosure document without furnishing the prospective franchisee with a copy of each revised agreement at least seven calendar-days before the prospective franchisee signs the revised agreement."

Although the FTC rule requires the material facts of the franchise offering to be disclosed in writing, it does not require franchisors to register or file the offering with the FTC or any other federal agency.

Disclosure Requirements

The disclosure document required by the FTC was originally modeled after the Uniform Franchise Offering Circular, or UFOC, designed to comply with individual state franchise investment laws, as related in Chapter 2. The federally prescribed document is known formally as the Franchisor Disclosure Document, or FDD.

The FDD is required to contain information on the following subjects:

1. Identifying information about the franchisor
2. Business experience of the franchisor's directors and key executives

3. Litigation history of the franchisor or its directors and key executives
4. Bankruptcy history of the franchisor or its directors and key executives
5. Initial fees required to be paid by the franchisee
6. Other fees
7. Estimated total initial investment
8. Restrictions on sources of products and services
9. Franchisee's obligations
10. Description of any franchisor assistance in financing the business
11. Description of any franchisor assistance, advertising, computer Systems, or training
12. The territory granted to the franchisee
13. Trademarks owned by the franchisor or an affiliate
14. Patents, copyrights, and proprietary information owned by the franchisor or an affiliate
15. Franchisee's obligation to participate in the actual operation of the franchise business
16. Restrictions on what the franchisee may sell
17. Renewal, termination, transfer, and dispute resolution
18. Celebrity involvement with the franchise
19. Financial performance representations
20. Information about the franchisor's established outlets and franchisees
21. Franchisor's financial statements
22. Contracts
23. Receipts

The Amended Franchise Rule requires the disclosures to be written in plain English, which is defined as follows:

"...the organization of information and language usage understandable by a person unfamiliar with the franchise business. It incorporates short sentences; definite, concrete, everyday language; active voice; and tabular presentation

of information, where possible. It avoids legal jargon, highly technical business terms, and multiple negatives."

If earnings claims are made, the information must be presented in a prescribed format and accompanied by a footnote cautioning prospective franchisees. It should be noted that franchisors are not specifically required to make any earnings claims. In fact, about half of all franchisors take advantage of this loophole and do not make any earnings claims in Item 19 o f the disclosure document.

All of the required disclosures must be made in a single document, which may not include any other information not prescribed by the Rule. Whenever a material change occurs in the information required to be disclosed, a quarterly revision is required to be prepared.

The Time for the Making of Disclosures

The FTC rule defines the "time for making of disclosures" as "at least 14 calendar-days before the prospective franchisee signs a binding agreement with or makes any payment to the franchisor or an affiliate."

Simply stated, no franchise agreement or any related contract may be executed, or any payment accepted by the franchisor, until the 14-day waiting period has lapsed. If the agreement is revised, the amended contract must be provided to the prospective franchisee at least seven days before signing.

Note the phrase "any consideration in connection" with the franchise. Remember it well when you enter the franchisor's conference room to sit down with the franchise sales representative.

FRANCHISE DISCLOSURE DOCUMENT

Widget World Franchise Corp.
An Arizona Corporation
1924 N. Central Ave.
Phoenix, Arizona 85436

(602) 222-3333
admin@widgetworld.com
www.widgetworld.com

Widget World Franchise Corp. operates retail establishments known as Widget World Stores. The total investment necessary to begin operation of a Widget World franchise is $165,300. This includes $17,500 that must be paid to the franchisor or affiliate.

This disclosure document summarizes certain provisions of your franchise agreement and other information in plain English. Read this disclosure document and all agreements carefully. You must receive this disclosure document at least 14 calendar days before you sign a binding agreement with, or make any payment to, the franchisor or an affiliate in connection with the proposed franchise sale.

Note, however, that no government agency has verified the information contained in this document.

Optional: You may wish to receive your disclosure document in another format that is more convenient to you. To discuss the availability of disclosures in different forms, contact Widget World franchise administration at 1924 N. Central Ave., Phoenix, Arizona 85436 and (602) 222-3333.

The terms of your contract will govern your franchise relationship. Do not rely on the disclosure document alone to understand your contract. Read all of your contract carefully. Show your contract and this disclosure document to an advisor, like a lawyer or an accountant.

Buying a franchise is a complex investment. The information in this disclosure document can help you make up your mind. More information on franchising, such as "A Consumer's Guide to Buying a Franchise," which can help you understand how to use this disclosure document, is available from the Federal Trade Commission. You can contact the FTC at 1-877-FTC-HELP or by writing to the FTC at 600 Pennsylvania Avenue, NW, Washington, DC 20580. You can also visit the FTC's home page at www.ftc.gov for additional information. Call your state agency or visit your public library for other sources of information on franchising.

There may also be laws on franchising in your state. Ask your state agencies about them.

Issued: April 15, 2018

Example of a FDD cover page

Unless you have had at least 14 days to study the FDD and the franchise agreement, no franchisor may ask, coerce, or encourage you to make any kind of payment. That includes any deposit, down payment, or purchase of inventory relating to the franchise.

Every professional salesperson knows well the meaning of the term "false urgency." A franchise salesman may create false urgency by telling you that several potential franchisees are waiting in line for the same territory. But if he asks for a deposit to "hold" the franchise before the waiting period has elapsed, the salesman could be held in violation of the Amended Franchise Rule.

Penalties for Violation

The Federal Trade Commission Act declares unlawful any "unfair methods of competition in commerce, and unfair or deceptive acts or practices in commerce." The Amended Franchise Rule cites this law and further declares that "it is an unfair or deceptive act or practice" for a franchisor to fail to abide by the prescribed disclosure requirements. Specifically, it is a federal crime to fail to furnish the prescribed disclosure document to any prospective franchisee, within the time frames established by the Rule. A franchisor that violates the FTC rules may be subject to civil penalties of up to $10,000 per violation. Moreover, an investor who sustains losses as a result of a violation of the federal rules will be awarded monetary damages.

The Right of Rescission

What if a franchisor should happen to pressure you into signing an agreement before the required waiting period has elapsed? Or what if a franchise salesman fails to give you a disclosure document on the day of your first personal meeting with a franchise sales representative?

Though it's a federal crime to violate an FTC rule, it's not very likely a guilty franchisor will be led off in chains. If a franchisor, franchise salesman, or broker fails to abide the regulations, the franchisee may have the right to rescind any agreement. In addition, the franchisee will normally be entitled to full compensation for the total amount of the investment, plus any damages that can be proved in court.

The FDD and the FTC Rules

There are differences in the form of disclosure required by the FTC's Amended Franchise Rule and the original UFOC adopted by individual states that regulate the offering and sale of franchises.

The UFOC generally fulfilled the requirements of the states that have laws requiring franchise registration and disclosure. The UFOC format is similar but not identical to the disclosure format prescribed by the federal rule. Besides minor differences in language, the state-mandated UFOC requires more disclosure on some subjects than the FTC rules.

However, the two formats are quite similar and designed to achieve the same result, regardless of the minor variations. Thus, until July 1, 2008, the FTC considered that the UFOC fulfilled the disclosure requirements of the Franchise Rule, provided that the franchisor complied with the prescribed time frames. After that date, only the newer Franchise Disclosure Document could be used.

However, complying with the federal rules does not relieve the franchisor of the obligation to comply with any applicable state franchise investment laws. The courts have ruled that in instances where the state law is more strict than the FTC rule, the state law takes priority.

Exemptions from the FTC Rule

Franchises and other continuing commercial relationships that do not fall into the two categories defined by the FTC rule are exempt from the disclosure requirements. They are not, however, exempt from other aspects of the Federal Trade Commission Act which forbids "unfair and deceptive business practices."

For example, a franchise that does not cost the franchisee anything, or results in less than $570 during the first six months of operation, is not covered by the FTC rule.

A second type of exemption is granted to fractional franchises (ones that account for less than 20% of the franchisee's total dollar volume). To qualify as a fractional franchise, the franchisee's directors or executive officers must have at least two years experience in the type of business in which the franchise is engaged.

The Amended Rule exempts any franchise sale in which the franchisee's initial investment is at least $1,143,100, excluding the cost of unimproved land and any financing provided by the franchisor or an affiliate. The reasoning is that an investor capable of putting up the threshold amount has sufficient financial knowledge to make a responsible decision without the benefit of a detailed disclosure document.

This exemption focuses on the level of the initial investment, not on the number or type of outlets being sold. Investors are prohibited from pooling their funds to fulfill the initial investment requirement. Where a group of investors seeks to purchase a franchise, at least one individual must invest the minimum threshold amount or more, for the exemption to apply.

The FTC adjusts the amount of the monetary threshold every four years, based on the Consumer Price Index calculated by the U.S. Department of Labor. When the

Amended Rule was originally implemented, the threshold amount was $1 million.

It should be noted, however, that an exemption from the federal rules does not exempt a franchisor from its obligations under applicable state franchise investment laws.

State Regulation of Franchise Sales

In 1971, California became the first state to enact a franchise investment law requiring registration by franchisors. The law requires that, before offering franchises in the state, a franchisor must file an application with the Department of Corporations and await approval.

Section 31114 of that law declares:

"The application for registration shall be accompanied by a proposed offering prospectus, which shall contain the material information set forth in the application..."

The referenced "offering prospectus" was later adopted by a consortium of midwestern securities commissioners as the Uniform Franchise Offering Circular, or UFOC, a standardized document designed to fulfill the requirements of various state franchise investment laws.

In brief, the prospectus discloses pertinent information about the franchisor, the franchise business, and the franchise agreement. Franchisors are specifically required to emphasize any areas that might have a negative impact on franchisees.

Fourteen other states, commonly called the "registration states," have since enacted similar laws calling for the registration of franchise offerings and the filing of disclosure documents.

The application for registration of a franchise in a regulated state consists of four basic parts: (1) a facing page, (2) a supplemental information page, (3) a salesman disclosure form, and (4) a copy of the proposed disclosure document.

Some states, including California, also require franchisors to submit copies of any proposed advertising materials that will be used to promote franchise opportunities. In most instances, both the registration and the advertisements must be approved by the regulatory agency before the franchisor may proceed. The state franchise investment laws also stipulate a waiting period, usually ten business days, after the UFOC is furnished to a prospective franchisee and before a sale is made.

Failure to register can result in criminal as well as civil penalties. In 1988, an Illinois court ruled that the executives of a franchise organization can be held personally liable for registration and disclosure violations under that state's Franchise Disclosure Act.

It is important to remember that approval of a registration by a state agency does not in any way constitute approval or endorsement of a franchisor's offering.

The following states currently regulate the offer and sale of franchises. In many of these states, the regulations are more strict than those of the FTC.

California
Hawaii
Illinois
Indiana
Maryland
Michigan
Minnesota
New York
North Dakota
Rhode Island
South Dakota
Virginia

Washington
Wisconsin

The following states have other laws that govern aspects of the franchisor-franchisee relationship:

Arkansas
California
Connecticut
Delaware
Hawaii
Illinois
Indiana
Iowa
Michigan
Minnesota
Mississippi
Missouri
Nebraska
New Jersey
North Dakota
South Dakota
Virginia
Washington
Wisconsin

Franchise Registration

A franchisor must apply with a government authority before offering franchises in a registration state. The application must be approved before any franchises may be offered or sold to any prospective franchisee in that state. Franchisors located in the state are also required to register, even they intend to sell franchises out of state.

No matter where the company's headquarters are located, the franchisor must register in your state of residence, if it happens to be one a registration state. This requirement applies even though the franchisor may be planning on opening the outlet in a different state. If the outlet will be located in a different registration state, the franchisor must register in that state, as well.

Fee Impoundment

If the state authorities do not find the franchisor's financial statement to be strong enough to fulfill all the promises and obligations created by the franchise agreement, they may impound franchise fees. Under an impoundment order, the franchisor must place the initial fee collected from a franchisee in an escrow account. The funds are released to the franchisor on a state order only after the franchisee signs a statement affirming that the franchisor has fulfilled all his promises and obligations.

So, anyone who purchases a franchise from a franchisor in a regulated state, if the franchisor's financial statements do not show a seven-figure net worth, may find himself or herself writing out a check to an impoundment account.

A franchise impoundment account is a type of escrow and, as such, may produce interest on any deposited funds. The terms of the impoundment stipulate that the monies will not be released to the franchisor until you, the franchisee, avow in writing that the franchisor has fulfilled all his promises and obligations to your personal satisfaction.

Authorization to Advertise Franchises for Sale

In many registration states, a franchisor may not place an advertisement to sell or promote a franchise until the state regulatory agency has reviewed and approved the ad. The law requires a franchisor to submit advertising materials, including brochures as well as newspaper or magazine ads, to a regulator, then wait five days for clearance. If no restraining order results, the franchisor may proceed with the ad campaign.

Periodic Updates

Franchisors approved by a regulated state must periodically update their applications in the form of bi-annual amendments. Even if no changes have occurred during the last six months, an update must normally be filed, in order to maintain the franchiser registration. Whenever a franchisor sells a franchise, changes a contract provision, or is involved in court activity, the disclosure document must be amended.

Besides state and federal regulations, the courts also influence the rights of franchisees when they rule on disputes. These decisions affect not only how a franchisor may offer and sell the franchise but the ground rules for purchasing, pricing, and involuntary termination.

State vs. Federal Regulations

In cases where a state regulation conflicts with a federal regulation, the courts have ruled that the state law takes precedence. *Dickey's Barbecue Restaurants, Inc. v. Chorley Enterprises, Inc.*, involved a franchisor seeking registration to sell franchises in the State of Maryland. The Maryland Franchise Law Regulations stipulate that a franchisor would be in violation of the law if it required a franchisee to "waive the franchisee's right to file a lawsuit alleging a cause of action arising under the Maryland Franchise Law in any court of competent jurisdiction in this State." However, the Dickey's franchise agreement required all disputes to be arbitrated, thereby waiving the franchisee's right to sue.

The courts determined that the waiver was illegal under Maryland law and that the franchisor had the choice of either complying with the state law or not selling franchises in the state.

7
INSIDE THE FRANCHISE DISCLOSURE DOCUMENT

"In their vanity men focus on what they wish to hear and miss the hidden meaning, the lurking threat."
                                                    David Hewson

Although the FDD informs prospective franchisees about the proposed investment, it does not completely shield them from potential fraud. The burden of verifying a franchisor's credentials and credibility remains with the franchisee. So don't rely on the FDD alone; if any gaps appear in the disclosures, ask for a complete resume of each of the principals, covering their entire business history. The Federal Trade Commission requires all U.S. franchisors to disclose certain information to the public. In cases where the local law or regulation is more severe than the FTC rule, the local restrictions take precedence. As we saw in Chapter Seven, the state rules apply whenever one of the following is true:

- The franchisor is headquartered in the regulated state.
- The franchisor plans to offer or sell franchises in the regulated state.
- A franchise outlet will be opened in the regulated state.

- A person who purchases a franchise is a resident of the regulated state, even though the outlet may be opened in another state.

What about franchisors headquartered in one of the states that do not require registration? When they offer or sell franchises to people who live in unregulated states, the important requirements are preparing a FDD and complying with the FTC's mandated waiting period.

The Disclosure Document

The FDD's purpose is to disclose vital information about a franchise opportunity. It presents highlights of the franchise agreement and describes the backgrounds of the franchisor and his associates.

However, often what is said in an disclosure document is not as important as what is not said. An omission of a pertinent fact is a form of inaccuracy and a violation of the full and accurate disclosure requirement. Nevertheless, omissions do occur, and it is usually difficult to prove in a court of law that they were made with an intent to defraud. Moreover, a FDD is not policed with the same rigor as, say, a securities prospectus.

The amended Rule requires franchisors to disclose the specified information clearly, legibly, and concisely in a single document, using plain English.

To shed light on how to evaluate a disclosure document and how to search between the lines for disguised or hidden meanings, we will examine each section of the FDD separately.

1. The Franchisor and Any Parents, Predecessors, and Affiliates

The first section is devoted to the franchisor's personal and business names, address, organization, background, and financial history. Any parents or predecessors of the franchising company must also be listed.

Under the amended Rule, a "parent" means "an entity that controls another entity directly, or indirectly though one or more subsidiaries." The term includes *all* parents in the chain of ownership, not just the immediate parent-owner of the franchisor, and not just the "ultimate" or "highest" parent in a chain of ownership.

A "predecessor" means a previous business operated by the franchisor which has a direct relationship to the franchise.

Consider, as an example, a franchisor who once owned a taxicab company before starting a successful toy store. After a few years, he decides to package a franchise program based on his retail toy operation. So, he founds a new company to sell toy store franchises.

In the FDD, the franchisor must disclose that he owned the original toy store, because that business was a predecessor to the franchising company. But he does not have to disclose his involvement in the taxicab business, since that operation has no relation to the toy store franchise.

Most franchising companies are operated as separate business entities from their original operations. Assume, for example, that an entrepreneur owns a successful health food restaurant, and he decides to begin selling franchises. He starts a new business whose only activity will be franchising. As a result, he now owns two separate businesses: a health food restaurant and a franchising company.

The reason a franchisor creates a separate franchising company is to limit his risks. If the franchising business runs into trouble, the original operation may not fail or even be liable for the losses or damages incurred by the franchising operation.

The issue of predecessor companies raises several important questions:

. How long has the franchisor operated a business similar to the proposed franchise outlet?

. What kind of success did the franchisor experience in the business?

. Can that success be duplicated in your locality?

. Were any of the principals involved in an enterprise that might suggest ethical impropriety, poor judgment, or just bad management?

A franchisor with nothing to hide will most likely list all the companies founded or owned prior to developing the franchise.

In addition to his predecessor companies, the franchisor must describe the business of the franchise, the types of customers for this type of product or service, and the competition.

2. Business Experience

The identity and business experience of the directors, trustees, partners, principals, and other managers of the franchising company must also be disclosed in this section. A short biography of each person states name, position, and experience for the last five years.

Note that the rules require a background disclosure for only the five years previous to the effective date of the disclosure document.

For example, assume the vice president of a franchising company was hired three years ago. For the prior three years, he was an executive with a large corporation in the same industry. But before that, he ran a side show for a traveling carnival. Under the franchise rules, only the officer's business background for the past five years has to be disclosed. So, the FDD would have to list only his positions as vice president of the franchising company and as a corporate executive in the industry. Because his carnival show period took place more than five years ago, this entire episode may lawfully be omitted from the FDD. Yet, that fact, if disclosed, might very well influence your final decision whether or not to purchase a franchise from this company.

Moreover, California law actually forbids the disclosure of any criminal arrest or conviction. So, it's possible even for a convicted rapist or a bank robber to appear flawless on a franchise disclosure document.

Franchisors who really are squeaky clean are more likely to publish a full declaration of each principal's criminal, financial, and business background in the FDD, above and beyond the legal time limits for disclosure. If a franchisor's disclosures stick closely to the limits, it's wise not to rely on the FDD alone to assess such information.

Ask the franchise representative for the complete resumes of all the individuals listed in the disclosure document. Bluntly inquire if any of them have ever been sued or declared bankrupt. Your franchisor may decline to answer, but might be against the law for him or any of his representatives or brokers to lie to you about this, or any other matter related to the franchise. If you don't get the information you ask for, and you feel it's important, you can always break off negotiations and look for a different franchise.

3. Litigation

Under the amended Franchise Rule, lawsuits falling into four categories must be disclosed in this section: pending lawsuits, lawsuits involving the franchise relationship, prior lawsuits, and current government injunctive or restrictive actions. These include arbitration proceedings.

Ordinarily, mediations need not be disclosed, unless the mediation resulted in the settlement of an ongoing lawsuit that must be disclosed. It also includes foreign litigation, even if the actions are in a foreign court or arbitration forum.

The franchisor must describe any criminal or civil actions involving any violation of a franchise law, fraud, embezzlement, or unfair business practices. But any lawsuit which did not specifically involve one of these violations does not have to be disclosed in the FDD. Since California law forbids the disclosure of a criminal record, in that state only civil actions will appear in a FDD.

When a criminal or civil action is disclosed, the FDD must reveal the title and parties of the action, the court, the nature of the claim, and the relationship between the litigating parties. If there is no pending litigation, that, too, should be stated.

In an age of widespread and often casual litigation, the question arises: just how extensive must these disclosures be? Can they be limited to those cases that are pertinent to the franchise business?

For example, assume you're the vice president of a franchise corporation and you sell your house to relocate. Several months after escrow closes, the buyer discovers a leak in the roof. Disgruntled, he sues you for fraud, claiming you knew the roof leaked all along. You, of course, claim you had no prior knowledge of the leak. But until the matter is settled, the litigation remains on the books. Does this case have to be included in the franchise disclosure document?

The rules are clear on this issue. For the franchisor or any director, trustee, partner, officer, financial, marketing, training, or service executive, the disclosure document must describe any pending administrative, criminal or material civil action

> . . . *alleging a violation of any franchise law, fraud, embezzlement, fraudulent conversion, misappropriation of property or comparable allegations.*

Note the rule says "alleging." Even while the case is in dispute, the particulars have to be disclosed. In addition, the FDD must describe any felony conviction or court injunction relating to the franchise in the last ten years.

4. Bankruptcy

In this section, the franchisor must reveal whether he, any predecessor in the business, or any of his partners or officers have been declared bankrupt in the last fifteen years. Specifically, he must tell whether any of the foregoing have been

> *". . . adjudicated bankrupt or reorganized due to insolvency."*

If an individual was an officer or partner in a company that went bankrupt, that, too, must be disclosed. Because personal bankruptcies are so prevalent under present law, it is not uncommon for a franchisor to have at least one principal or executive who has undergone the process of insolvency.

For example, the franchise sales director for a well-known franchisor in the transportation field once owned a small shoe store which fell on hard times during the nationwide recession of the late 1970s. But that bankruptcy had no bearing whatsoever on his performance as a sales director for his current employer. So, even though the incident was recorded in the company's FDD, it was not likely to influence a prospective franchisee's decision.

It is important to realize that just because a franchisor has in his employ an executive who once declared bankruptcy does not by itself doom the franchise to failure. But beware of the franchisor who attempts to disguise a past bankruptcy rather than openly disclose it.

5. *Initial Fees*

This section of the FDD states the amount of the franchise fee. The disclosure should also describe the franchisor's provisions for refunds, and state whether the fee is payable in a lump sum or in installments.

For example, some franchise agreements do not allow for the initial fee to be refunded under any conditions. Others provide for fifty percent of the fee to be refunded if the franchisee fails to pass the franchisor's training program. Whereas some franchisors demand the entire initial fee be paid in a single lump sum when the franchise agreement is signed, others will accept or defer partial payments.

The franchisor must also state where the initial fee will end up; usually, it is deposited in the" general funds" of the franchising company. It's common for an disclosure document to say that the initial fee is "fully earned by the franchisor." Simply stated, that means when you sign the franchise agreement and pay the initial fee, you agree that you are not entitled to a refund if you decide to back out later.

6. *Other Fees*

Any other fees or payments, such as the ongoing royalty or advertising fund, must be disclosed in this section of the FDD. If, after signing a franchise agreement, you end up having to pay special charges or fees not specifically disclosed in the FDD, there's a possibility your franchisor may have violated the law.

To illustrate, let's say you are considering investing in a franchise for a family-style restaurant. Recognizing that location is important to success in this line of business, the franchisor agrees to select the site for your outlet. Two weeks after you sign the franchise agreement, a representative arrives in your hometown to scout out the trading area. Aided by local real estate consultants, the franchise representative finally picks the "perfect" site for your new restaurant. He even stays around long enough to help you negotiate the lease. Two weeks later, you receive a bill for the representative's air fare, lodging, food, and a "site selection fee."

In cases like this example, the site selection fee and all related charges must be listed in the FDD for you to inspect before you sign the agreement. Likewise, any similar charges for consultation services, accounting, marketing, or other assistance should be fully and accurately disclosed.

7. *Estimated Initial Investment*

This section of the disclosure document breaks down your total initial investment. The breakdown must say exactly who receives each payment item and when it is due.

For example, the initial fee is payable to the franchisor, and it is usually due "on signing" the franchise agreement. But a lease deposit for your store or office is paid to your lessor, due" as agreed" by you and the lessor. If the lessor of the site happens to be your franchisor, that fact will appear in this section of the FDD.

When the initial investment is likely to vary e.g., due to local economic conditions a high-low estimate is often made. The high estimate includes the highest initial fee charged by the franchisor, as well maximum amounts for such items as real estate, equipment, and supplies. The low estimate reflects the lowest investment for which a franchisee could conceivably get into the business. However, the low investment breakdown is usually based on costs found only in certain areas of the country, i.e., the most economically depressed markets.

The breakdown may include the cost of real estate, equipment, fixtures, inventory, deposits, or other payments. Figure 81 shows an example of a franchisor's estimated initial investment breakdown. The illustration gives an amount for working capital; this figure represents the estimated cash required to sustain the business until it begins to turn a profit. Franchisors are not specifically required to include working capital as part of the initial investment breakdown.

If you are considering a franchise and the estimated investment does not include working capital requirements, be sure to ask the franchisor for a low-high estimate. By omitting working capital, the franchisor produces a seemingly lower cost of getting into the franchise; but it is impossible to start a business without an amount set aside for working capital.

8. Restrictions on Sources of Products or Services

In this section of the FDD, franchisors must disclose whether you will be required to buy any products, equipment, or services either from the franchisor or from a specified source. For example, if you obtain a franchise to open a muffler shop, will you have to purchase and sell only mufflers offered by your franchisor? If you don't have to buy them from your franchisor, will be you forced to buy them from a particular supplier? If so, what is the supplier's connection (if any) with your franchisor?

It is difficult, but not impossible, for a franchisor to force franchisees to purchase equipment, supplies, or inventory from a designated source. In the past, the courts have frowned on such soles-source purchasing obligations, unless it can be proved that the product is so unique it cannot be obtained from any other supplier.

For instance, let's say you're considering a franchise to open an internet cafe. The franchisor cannot usually force you to purchase computers from either the franchisor or the franchisor's designated supplier. But he can force you to comply with his specifications for type and quality. You're free to purchase computers from any supplier. But the chances are good that your franchisor or his designated source will offer the best combination of availability and pricing. Most franchisors encourage their franchisees to purchase from a designated source by offering discount pricing or other benefits.

9. Franchisee's Obligations

This section of the FDD must disclose whether, as a franchisee, you will be required to buy any products or supplies based on the franchisor's specifications or prior approval. For instance, assume you are considering a franchise to start a computer store, and the franchisor requires that you sell only computers that appear on his "approved product" list. That requirement must be disclosed before you sign the franchise agreement, not after you begin setting up your showroom.

Purchasing standards are usually designed to encourage franchisees to buy particular brands or to use a particular supplier. For example, if you own an ice cream parlor franchise, your franchisor cannot force you to carry only a certain brand of ice cream. What he can do is stipulate a set of specifications that conform to a particular make or model. You have the choice of carrying the product line which conveniently meets the franchisor's specifications, or, as an alternative, investing a few million dollars to manufacture your own version. Now, which option is more attractive?

10. Financing

This section of the FDD is used to describe any financing arrangements offered by the franchisor or another party associated with the franchise. Many franchisors offer financial assistance to franchisees. Some will finance all or part of your investment, others only the initial fee.

A franchising company that does not offer its own financing arrangement often has ties with a local bank or investment company. For example, let's say you want to buy a franchise, but you'll need a bank loan to swing the deal. The franchisor you have in mind doesn't offer financing, but during your visit to franchise headquarters, you are introduced to an officer of a nearby bank. To your surprise, the banker has already transferred all your financial data from the franchise application onto a loan application. "All you have to do," the loan officer assures you, "is sign."

Sound easy? Maybe too easy, you might think. The bank in this example probably handles all the franchisor's banking business. The franchisor may even have agreed to cosign for the loan. In some cases, the franchisor receives a commission or "finder's fee" for sending the bank new business.

No matter what the arrangement, the details must be disclosed in the FDD.

11. Franchisor's Assistance, Advertising, Computer Systems and Training

Under this heading, the franchisor describes the service he promises to provide you after you sign the franchise agreement. The list of services is broken down as follows:

a. Services provided prior to opening
b. Other supervision or assistance

c. Services provided while you are open for business
d. Assistance in selecting the site for your outlet

Also in this section, the franchisor must disclose the location and length of the training program, and states exactly who must pay for the travel and living expenses. It may surprise you to learn that most franchisees must pay for their own airline tickets, hotel rooms, and meals while they are attending franchise training school. If that's the case, this obligation must be clearly stated in the FDD.

A typical franchise training program lasts from one to three weeks. Unless you live in the franchisor's hometown, the cost of travel, lodging, and meals is likely to be considerable. Yet, this cost is often excluded from the initial investment breakdown in Section 6 of the FDD. If you are required to pay for your own transportation and lodging to attend the training program, the FDD should state a reasonable estimate of the *per diem*, or daily cost.

The following example is extracted from Section 11 of an actual FDD:

> *Franchisee is required to pay his own costs in connection with attending the training program. The cost per diem, including lodging and meals, is likely to be ninety dollars ($90) per day.*

Like the low estimate in the initial investment breakdown, the cost per diem is usually based on budget lodging and inexpensive restaurants. Although you may actually be able to contain your travel costs within this estimate, chances are you won't find the accommodations satisfactory or the meals appetizing. As a general rule, it's a good idea to multiply the franchisor's estimate for lodging and meals by one and a half.

12. Territory

In this section of the FDD, the franchisor must state whether or not you will receive a protected territory as part of your franchise. Will you receive an exclusive territory? Does the franchisor promise not to sell any other franchises in your territory? Can the franchisor sell the same products to customers in your territory by mail order or through any other means?

Territories don't always come with a franchise. When they do, their boundaries may be subject to change. For instance, if you have a franchise to sell cosmetics in a designated part of the city, you might be obligated to maintain a certain sales volume. If you fail to meet the quota, you may find your territory shrinking in size. On the other hand, if you happen to exceed the sales quota, your franchisor might see fit to expand your territorial boundaries.

The concept of an exclusive franchise territory is widely misunderstood. By granting a territory, the franchisor is simply agreeing not to compete with the franchisee by selling other franchises or placing company sales representatives in the territory. Franchisors do not, and cannot, assure franchise buyers that other franchisees will not sell to customers in the same territory.

As independent business owners, franchisees are free to sell to any customers anywhere they like, including customers situated in another franchisee's territory. That freedom applies equally to the franchisee's territory as well as to those of neighboring franchisees.

13. Trademarks

In this section of the FDD, the franchisor must disclose what steps he has taken to protect the use of the franchise name, trademarks, and symbols. The most obvious step is to register the name or mark with the federal government.

The franchisor must list and describe all logos, slogans, or other commercial symbols associated with the franchise. If there is art work involved in the registered logo or trademark, it should be reproduced in the FDD.

You should note that franchisors do not always own the exclusive rights to their own trade marks. For example, the trade mark may simply be "applied for," not registered. In that instance, you may run the risk of losing the right to use the trade mark if for some reason the registration should be denied.

On the other hand, there is a lengthy period during which every trade mark is only "applied for," before registration is finally granted. This status is by no means a cause for discounting a franchise opportunity. But a fully registered trade mark is clearly more valuable than one that is still under application. Until the registration has been approved by the U. S. Registrar of Trade Marks, there remains a risk, no matter how small, that the name or mark will not be protected.

Be sure the trade name or trade mark has been registered with the federal government, not just with a city or state agency. Protection of a trade name in the franchisor's home town is useless in your area unless it is backed by federal registration.

14. *Patents, Copyrights, and Proprietary Information*

Under this heading, the franchisor must list any special patents or copyrights that are "material" to the value of the franchise. If a franchise is supposed to be based on a unique patent or design, look in this section of the FDD to find the patent number, date, and description. If this information is missing, you might ask yourself whether the product or design is really "unique."

15. Obligation to Participate in the Actual Operation of the Business

In this section of the disclosure document, the franchisor must state whether the person who buys the franchise must run the business himself, or whether he may hire someone else to manage it for him. Many franchisors sell to "absentee" owners who do not actively participate in the management of the business.

If you are investing in a franchise as a "silent" partner, be sure you know whether the franchisor permits absentee partnership. If you intend to hire someone else to manage the business, check to see that the disclosure document specifically discloses the franchisor's permission to do so.

16. Restrictions on What the Franchisee May Sell

It must be disclosed in this section if franchisees will be limited or restricted in any way as to the type of products and services they may sell. For instance, if someone buys a franchise to sell exercise equipment door to door, can the franchisor prevent the franchisee from selling encyclopedias at the same time? Or will a person planning to open a computer store franchise be able to sell copy machines and office furniture as well?

On the surface, this issue may not seem important. But if you already own a convenience store franchise and you're considering a second franchise to sell hot dogs or flavored ice on the premises, you had better be certain the franchises are compatible under the provisions of both franchise agreements.

17. Renewal, Termination, Transfer, and Dispute Resolution

This section of the FDD spells out the provisions of the franchise agreement dealing with your right to renew the franchise when the contract expires; how the agreement can be involuntarily terminated by either party; whether the franchisor has the right of first refusal to repurchase the franchise; and any restrictions governing assignment of the contract to someone other than the person who originally bought the franchise.

We'll take a closer look at these important issues in Chapter 13, when we translate a franchise agreement into plain language.

18. Public Figures

In this section, the franchisor must disclose all the details behind any arrangement to use the name and reputation of a public figure. For instance, let's say you are considering a franchise to start a fast food restaurant with the name of someone called Granny Opry on the sign. Just exactly how is Granny associated with the business? How much is the franchisor paying her to use her name? Unless these facts were disclosed, you might think Granny actually owns the franchising company.

Franchisors sometimes pay famous sports figures, singers, or movie stars to put their names on a franchise offering. Some of these public figures own stock in the franchising corporation, but others have no ownership participation at all.

19. Financial Performance Representations

This section of the disclosure document is used to predict how much you can expect to make in the business. The prediction must be accompanied by the formula used to calculate the projected profits or earnings. No matter how the projections are made, the franchisor must inform you that there is no assurance that you can actually attain such sales levels or earnings.

An earnings projection can only be safely made when the franchisor actually has a large number of outlets that have been open for many years. Even then, the projections should be considered hypothetical, since economic conditions vary greatly from one geographic area to the next.

A far more reliable projection is your own forecast of the economic potential of the business, based partly on information contained in the FDD, but also on accurate estimates of costs and expenses in your locality. A step-by-step guide to projecting the franchise's potential profits will be described later in this volume.

20. Outlets and Franchisee Information

This section is used to list the number of franchises currently sold and open, their names and addresses, and an estimate of the total number to be granted in the forthcoming year in each state. If a franchisor has problems with franchise terminations, lawsuits, or other disputes, these must be disclosed here.

A new franchisor with no outlets can simply estimate the number to be sold in each state within the 12 months after the effective date of the offering circular.

Before making a final decision to purchase a franchise, it's wise for a potential investor to contact some established franchisees.

21. Financial Statements

A copy of the franchisor's current, audited financial statement must be attached to the circular. The rules do not allow any franchisor to substitute an unaudited financial statement of any kind. The financial statement must be audited by a certified public accountant whose official stamp appears on the document, and must be current within six months of the effective date of the disclosure document.

22. Contracts

A copy of the franchise agreement should be attached to the FDD. If there are any other related agreements, such as a purchase contract or lease agreement, each of these should be included, as well.

23. Receipts

The amended Rule requires franchisors to obtain a signed receipt for the disclosure document furnished to each prospective franchisee. The signature includes not only a handwritten signature, but the use of security codes, unique passwords, electronic signatures, or similar means of authentication.

Two copies of the receipt must be placed at the end of the disclosure document: one that the franchisee retains as part of the disclosure document, and the other that the franchisee must return to the franchisor.

Reading Between the Lines

Although the FDD is intended to shield prospective investors against fraudulent business practices, no official regulatory body checks the accuracy of the information. Even in states with strict regulations, the franchise authorities have neither the staff nor the budget to verify the contents of the thousands of FDDs which cross their desks each year.

8
INSIDE THE FRANCHISE DECISION

"We all make choices, but in the end our choices make us."
                                        Ken Levine

In 2001, two sisters who were intent on starting their own business entered into discussions with a franchisor of day care centers. The prospective franchisees received a *pro forma* earnings claim, which, according to the franchisor, was based on the actual income and expenses of franchise outlets that were already in operation. Impressed by the financial projections, the sisters decided to purchase the franchise offering. At a personal meeting, the franchisor gave the sisters a 17-page "Franchise Offering Circular for Prospective Franchisees for Non–Registration States" and a 37-page franchise agreement with a term of 25 years.

During the meeting, the franchisor pressured them to sign the documents that day, or risk losing the franchise. As a result, the applicants did not have time to read the documents or consult with an attorney before signing them. After signing the circular, the agreement, and an amendment to the agreement, they also paid a $30,000 franchise fee.

Ultimately, the two sisters invested more than $2.2 million in the franchise. They opened their daycare center 14 months after signing the agreement. By the end of the first year, they had lost over $200,000. Two years later, the outlet began to turn a profit, but the earnings were still far less than those stated on the earnings claim they had received from the franchisor. The franchisees' complaints were countered by the franchisor's claim that other daycare franchises were "doing fine," and it was the sisters' own fault that their center was not succeeding.

Upon investigation, the sisters discovered that four other franchisees in the network had nearly identical experiences. Each had been given an earning claim which, according to the franchisor, was based on the actual earnings of existing outlets. Each had also been told to sign the franchise agreement and pay the initial fee immediately, or risk losing the location.

On the surface, it may seem obvious that the franchisor in this case was at fault for ignoring the federal regulations governing full and accurate disclosure. In fact, based upon the evidence presented, a jury rendered a general verdict in favor of the sisters and found the franchisor personally liable for the judgments. However, because the franchisees had not exercised due diligence by reading the offering circular and franchise agreement, a higher court overturned the verdict and ordered the case to be retried.

In his ruling, the judge, wrote

> "The law will not excuse [a plaintiff] for failing to read the instrument . . . The law will protect the innocent against fraud . . . but it demands of every one that he make use of his own facilities to avoid being defrauded."

In essence, because the franchisees signed an agreement for a huge investment without reading it or having it reviewed by an attorney, the court refused to award them financial damages for fraud.

This case underscores several important aspects of the franchise decision and the methods employed by franchisors to recruit franchisees.

Reverse Selling

A technique known as "reverse selling" is often used to motivate prospective franchisees to assume an active role in making an investment decision. To stimulate this behavior, a franchisor may pose a series of psychological obstacles that the prospect must overcome to obtain the franchise.

The obstacles may range from minor nuisances to significant commitments. For instance, as a prospect, you might be required to inquire about the franchise opportunity at your own expense. The reasoning behind this tactic is that someone who is unwilling to commit to even the small expense of a long-distance phone call is unlikely to invest in a franchise or, for that matter, to be successful in running one. There's a lot to be said for this idea.

On the opposite side of the reverse-selling coin, a franchisor who uses persuasive selling tactics may have something to hide. Most likely, he sells franchises to anyone willing to buy one. Beware of the franchisor who makes it too easy to buy a franchise.

Understanding how buying decisions are made is helpful to organizing the research that should precede any franchise decision. It will also help you understand how franchisors recruit and motivate franchisees.

Buying decisions may be viewed in three basic categories: complex, low-involvement, and repetitive.

Complex Buying Decisions

Selecting a franchise from a wide field of potential opportunities is an example a complex buying decision. Such a decision may involve numerous factors that must be carefully evaluated before a transaction will take place. A complex buying decision has five stages:

1. Need arousal
2. Information processing
3. Evaluation
4. Selection
5. Outcome

Need arousal means recognizing that you have a need or want to be fulfilled. This is the first step in making any decision, no matter whether it is simple or complex. The instant you say to yourself "I want to start a business," you have become a prospective franchisee.

Behind virtually every franchise decision is the basic need for financial growth. A desire for a change of occupation or employment is sometimes important in need arousal. For example, some franchise opportunities attract investors who simply are bored with their present jobs.

Information Processing

After identifying your needs, you are ready to initiate a search for the available solutions. One way is to gather the information deliberately—for example, by contacting a franchise broker or consulting a directory of franchise opportunities. Information may also be received incidentally—for example, from an advertisement, internet blog, or magazine article.

Information processing consists of three basic phases:

1. Specification
2. Information gathering
3. Comprehension

Before beginning to gather information, you must break down your overall needs into more specific needs. What type of business do you have in mind? What size investment can you handle? Where do you want to locate the business? Your specific needs will immediately set the boundaries for the search process. Among other things, your needs will establish the investment range, a specific location, and, often, the type of business.

After specifying your needs, you are ready to begin gathering information. One way prospective investors gather information is by consulting reference sources such as a business journal or a directory of franchise opportunities.

In states that regulate franchise sales, a franchisee recruitment ad must pass bureaucratic inspection. Guarantees of success or vague claims of financial windfalls are specifically prohibited.

Franchisee recruitment ads appear every day in business and financial tabloids. The *Wall Street Journal* and *U.S.A Today* have classified advertising sections devoted specifically to franchise opportunities. Periodicals such as *Inc.*, *Venture*, and *Entrepreneur*, which also target people interested in starting a business, also run franchise ads. Some franchisors may run ads in a trade publication or special interest magazine to reach people experienced in a particular industry.

The example illustrates several psychological aspects of a typical recruitment marketing program. To cater to the reader's desire for self-esteem, the ad may refer to the franchise as the "president" or "owner" of his own business. After all, the word "franchisee" has a bland, legal sound, whereas the word "president" is dripping with prestige.

A recruitment ad is not an offering, and, except for the prohibition against false claims and success guarantees, the franchise company can say almost anything it wants. More reliable information can be gathered from sources such as *The Rating Guide to Franchises*, which condenses the franchise offering circulars of major franchisors and rates their opportunities according to such criteria as financial strength, fees and royalties, training and services, and industry experience.

Identifying opportunities is only the first step in information gathering. The next step is to request information kits from selected franchisors. We will take a close-up look at franchise information kits later in this chapter.

This step initiates the next phase of information processing—comprehension. Comprehension involves interpreting the information you have gathered and, if necessary, gathering additional data. For example, you might narrow the selection and then visit representative outlets to obtain empirical data about the franchise.

Empirical data is based on first-hand observation or experience, as opposed to merely reading or hearing about a product. In contrast, *perceptual data* is based on advertisements, reviews, or recommendations by other parties.

The Evaluation Phase

The evaluation stage of a complex buying decision takes place when you analyze your options. The options range from deciding not to invest to deciding on a particular franchise that seems to fulfill your needs. I use the term "seems to" here because evaluation is largely a matter of perception. For example, you may read a review in a magazine stating that a particular restaurant has excellent food, but, until you actually eat in that restaurant, the information is only perceptual.

Whether you realize it or not, your personal beliefs and attitudes have a strong influence on the evaluation process. For example, some people want to start a large business and are willing to invest more money. But others are mainly interested in a low investment and would be satisfied with a simple business. People who belong to certain religious or political organizations may give preference to franchises that are associated with their groups. Be aware that you have such influences, and try to determine how they will affect your selection decision.

Whether your attitudes are logical or not, they are important. If you are not entirely comfortable with your decision, or if you experience the slightest degree of negativity, will you have the total commitment it takes to succeed?

The Selection Phase

The selection phase occurs when you make a decision to proceed with one of the options. Usually, this phase consists of a series of smaller decisions. You might decide to reject all of the options, or, alternatively, you might decide to seek yet another solution. For example, if you were considering opening a family-style restaurant, you might decide to open a fast-food outlet instead.

As a prospective franchisee, the first selection you must make is the decision to proceed. A prospective franchisee enters the selection phase by requesting an information kit from one or more franchisors.

The Outcome

When a buying decision is made, the outcome may be either positive or negative. If the franchise adequately fulfills your overall and specific needs, and you are satisfied with the investment, the outcome may be considered positive.

In franchising, the true measurement of an outcome is franchisee satisfaction. With few exceptions, no franchisor cannot survive over the long term by selling only to new franchisees. A satisfied franchisee is a walking advertisement for the franchise, but a dissatisfied investor spreads ill will for the franchisor and all of its franchisees.

Low-Involvement Buying Decisions

In a low-involvement buying decision, the prospect is not highly involved in the information gathering, evaluation, or selection processes. An example is a business that has already been developed by the franchisor before it was offered as a franchise. Still, the final decision rests with the buyer, who might elect to invest in a different franchise. In this case, the search for an alternative franchise opportunity would have initiated a high-involvement buying decision.

Repetitive Buying Decisions

The example of the loyal customer who invested in her favorite franchise illustrates a repetitive buying decision. Most people do not regularly change their behavior, and this principle is also true of buying behavior. People adopt a regular pattern of behavior out of convenience. We learn from our experiences, and form our behavior on the basis of what we have learned. Thus, a satisfied customer has a reason to believe that his or her satisfaction will be repeated in the future.

Investing in a favorite franchise when the occasion arises transforms a complex buying decision into a relatively low-involvement decision.

Cultural Influences

Investors do not make franchise decisions solely on the basis of information processing and evaluation. They are also influenced by cultural factors, people, and lifestyle. Culture refers to the basic customs and beliefs of a community, religion, or ethnic group. The traits that characterize a particular culture are called cultural values and are passed from one generation to another. For example, in some Asian cultures, people consider cows to be sacred and, therefore, do not eat beef or dairy products. Most households in America have indoor toilets, and very few American travelers would select a hotel that does not have this feature. However, in some developing countries, indoor plumbing is found only in the residences of wealthy citizens, and, therefore, virtually any lodging establishment with a toilet is considered a first-class hotel. Yet, by American standards, the same property might be considered primitive or unacceptable.

More refined values exist within each culture. For example, in the United States, elderly people with fixed incomes often have different cultural values than a young, professional couple with children. Low-investment chains often direct their marketing efforts to families, retirees, and blue-collar individuals, whereas high-investment chains often focus on executives and affluent couples without children.

Be aware of the cultural influences that affect your investment decisions. They are a real part of you, and, as such, you cannot afford to ignore them. But also be aware that the business world is made up of people of diverse cultural backgrounds.

Reference Groups

Besides cultural values, prospective franchisees are also influenced by other people. The people who provide information or offer opinions that influence someone else's buying behavior are called a reference group. For example, a student is influenced by other people in his or her class, and an office worker receives information from co-workers. The most influential reference groups are families and friends.

Members of a reference group may be one of three basic types:

1. information sources
2. influencers
3. key decision makers

An information source is anyone who provides information that affects the investment decisions of others. For example, a happy franchisee may tell friends or relatives about his business. In this respect, every franchisee is an information source for other prospective franchisees.

An influencer is a person other than the prospective franchisee who has control over some aspect of the investment decision. Examples of influencers include family members, friends, business associates, and advisers such as an accountant, banker, or attorney.

A key decision maker is the person who is ultimately responsible for the investment decision. If the franchise will be owned by a corporation, the chief executive may be the key decision maker. In a family situation, marital bliss—and franchise success—may depend on both spouses sharing both the investment decision and the commitment to succeed.

A wise investor researches information sources and seeks the counsel of family, friends, associates, and professional advisors. If you are considering a franchise, realize that it is not your decision alone.

Whether your investment will be based on a complex, low-involvement, or repetitive decision, the adventure of starting and running a business will in some fashion affect your relationships with your family and your friends. Like the proverbial attorney who is a fool because he has himself for a lawyer, you would also be foolish not to seek out and rely upon qualified counsel.

The Lead Processing Labyrinth

After selecting a franchise and starting an investigation, you will open a door and enter a corridor. It will not be straight, like a tunnel, with a light visible at the end. Instead, it will continually branch in different directions and at times seem dimly lit. Like a lab mouse searching for a piece of cheese, it will take dedication, persistence, and possibly ingenuity to make your way through the labyrinth. A reward awaits you at the end, but only if you make all the right choices.

This weaving, branching, sometimes puzzling, maze enables the franchisor to select only those franchisees who have what it takes to make it in a franchise. Owning a business requires more than a desire to be one's own boss. It also requires a burning desire to succeed. In franchise brochures, that quality may be referred to as a "dedication to self-accomplishment," or the "willingness to do whatever it takes to succeed."

From a franchisor's point of view, every person who inquires about a franchise opportunity is a "lead." The labyrinth that leads from inquiring about a franchise to being offered a contract is called "lead processing." Franchisors reason that, if you don't have the perseverance to make it through the lead processing labyrinth, your chances of succeeding in a business are slim.

Lead processing begins when a prospect first inquires about a franchise opportunity—usually by dialing a telephone number or mailing a letter. The franchisor usually responds by mailing out an information package, referred to as a franchise "kit."

A typical kit contains a word-processed cover letter, a color brochure, reprints of newspaper or magazine articles about the franchise or industry, and a set of application forms. It may also include photographs and samples of product advertisements. Most franchisors wait until the applications are returned before offering circulars to selected prospects.

A franchise kit may tell you a great deal about the franchisor. To some extent, its depth, detail, preparation, and professionalism are telltale signs of the franchisor's own self-image, personality, and management skill.

A classic franchise kit consists of the following parts:

- History of the franchising company and its predecessor
- Overview of the franchise offering, stressing the benefits to franchisees
- Qualifications for becoming a franchisee
- Credibility devices, such as reprints of newspaper articles, sample ads, photographs, and product samples
- Application forms

The history is usually told in a brief and colorful description of the founding, growth, and development of the parent firm. What is said is often less relevant than what is not said. For example, a new franchise may be described as being "short on history," but "long on future." What this really means is the franchisor does not have much of a track record. When a franchise venture is so new that it has no history, the franchisor's hired ad men search their repertoire of superlatives to create convincing images. For example, you might find that, instead of the history of the company, the kit contains a history of the industry or possibly even the history of franchising.

The history of the franchisor often focuses on an individual, such as the founder of the company or a famous public figure associated with the franchise. The idea is that a franchisee can relate more easily to a human being than to a company. Franchisors know that, as a prospective franchisee, you will project your own identity into the business. The historical individual serves as a role model for you to follow. The premise of a "father figure" at the helm of the franchising corporation is an important element of many recruiting schemes.

The father figure exudes wisdom, inspires confidence, and warms the cockles of the heart. In some cases, it is a "grandmother" figure—the person who baked the first cookie, blended the first pizza sauce, or plucked the first chicken. In other cases, the figurehead may be a celebrity—for instance, a famous singer, actor, cowboy, or athlete.

Before you place too much faith in figureheads, it might pay to check on their background and credentials. Is he or she the real architect of the franchise, or just a token celebrity under contract to promote the business?

A typical franchise overview includes a breakdown of the initial investment. It may also enumerate the ostensible benefits of the franchise while only lightly touching upon the obligations and restrictions. These "negatives" are often left to the offering circular, which, in most cases, only the most highly qualified applicants receive.

Applicants for a franchise must contend with a glut of paper work, much of which may seem irrelevant on the surface. As discussed earlier, this documentation helps the franchisor ferret out tire kickers and motive those prospects who have a serious interest in the franchise. It also provides a concrete tool for testing a prospective franchisee's organizational and communication skills.

For example, how an individual answers an essay-type questionnaire reveals much about his character and personality. For example, if your answers seem poorly prepared, with no definite objective, the franchisor will think you are a poor organizer or a hesitant decision maker. If the answers are handwritten with bad grammar and incomplete sentences, you will be perceived as a poor communicator.

Worse, the franchisor may assume you have a poor self-image. If you don't care what kind of image your work conveys to others, what kind of image would you project for a franchise system?

In contrast, if your application forms are well thought out, neatly typed, grammatically correct, and concise but informative, you will be perceived as a competent organizer with solid communications skills and serious intent. What's more, you'll convey a high degree of confidence, self-image, and self-esteem.

If you were a franchisor, which type of applicant would you rather have as a franchisee?

A typical franchise application form usually consists of three parts: (1) personal data, (2) financial data, (3) references. A typical franchise application looks a lot like an employment application, with spaces for the applicant's name, personal and business address and telephone, birth date, and other personal data about the prospective franchisee. Most applications require the applicant to provide details regarding education and prior business background, including, names, places, dates, and degrees or titles.

To assess the applicant's financial capability or credit-worthiness, the application usually includes a financial questionnaire or statement of net worth. In this section, the prospective franchisee must document his or her assets, such as any equity in real estate holdings, personal property, and monies in savings and checking accounts; and liabilities, such as any outstanding loans or other debts, credit card balances, and taxes payable.

A typical franchisor will multiply the stated assets and net worth by 80 percent, to determine the amount that a conventional lending institution might be willing to lend the applicant. Usually, franchisors will have the financial information verified by an independent credit or background checking service.

The applicant's personal and professional references help the franchisor assess the prospective franchisee's work stability and esteem by others. Three references are commonly required, but in some instances as many as five to ten names may be requested.

As a final obstacle, most franchisors require serious applicants to visit the company's headquarters for a personal interview. You can expect the visit to be conducted at your own expense. If your residence is conveniently close to franchise headquarters, the franchisor might even move the interview to a less convenient location, just to see if you're willing to overcome this important barrier.

As discussed in Chapter Seven, a franchisor is required to provide you with a disclosure document, an audited financial statement, and a copy of the franchise agreement at least ten business days before you sign a contract. If you have not received these documents before your first meeting with a franchise representative, the franchisor must provide them at that time. For this reason, many franchisors will send you the legally prescribed documents about two weeks before you are scheduled to arrive at franchise headquarters.

In most cases, you will be required to sign and return a form acknowledging that you have received the documents, before the interview will be scheduled. This form is necessary to prove that the franchisor has complied with the rules and regulations.

The Recruitment Roller Coaster

After making it through the lead processing labyrinth, another door will open for you. Just outside, you will find a franchise representative waiting to strap you into the franchisor's emotional roller coaster.

The moment you send in a franchise application form, you cease to be a "lead" and become a "prospect." If you fit the ideal franchisee profile, if you qualify financially, and if your desired location or territory is available, you will be invited for a personal interview.

Most likely, when you arrive at franchise headquarters, your emotional state will be highly volatile. It will help you if you remember that most prospective franchisees undergo a series of emotional peaks and valleys. At one point, you'll be highly energetic, perhaps even wildly optimistic. At another, you'll be cautious, weary, perhaps even remorseful.

The franchisor may try to control your emotions. For example, at one point, you may view a videotape or slide presentation while seated in a comfortable, overstuffed leather chair. In this instance, the music and color are designed to stimulate your subconscious reactions, causing the roller coaster to climb. Some time later, you may sit down for an exhausting interview with a panel of department managers, setting off an emotional plunge.

Next may come a tour of a "typical" franchise outlet. In most cases, the tour will be scheduled during a period of peak customer activity. Some franchisors go so far as to hire fake "customers" to mingle in the outlet while a prospective franchisee is touring the facilities. In either case, the cash register will be constantly ringing, letting your imagination run wild with images of cascading greenbacks.

This new "high" may only precede a new "low" brought on by a dry, boring contract negotiation with a legal expert. If a franchisor is trying to manipulate your emotions, the contract will be presented for your signature when your spirits are on a sharp upturn. The closing always takes place on an optimistic peak, never in a remorseful valley.

As a prospective franchisee, you must try to maintain an even keel to prevent the franchisor's marketing experts from controlling your emotions and guiding your behavior. However, you should also recognize that buyer's remorse is a natural part of every major investment decision.

Sales pressure from a franchisor's sales staff can be extremely low key. You may not be pressured to sign; in fact, you may be discouraged. Again, this discouragement may be part of a reverse-selling strategy. The real aim may be to take away the franchise so that you'll scramble hurriedly to grab it back.

Above all, follow these simple rules:

1. Read the Franchise Disclosure Document (FDD) and Franchise Agreement.

2. Understand what you're agreeing to.

To make an intelligent decision, the best strategy is not to sign any agreement or to make any payment at the franchisor's place of business. Wait until you're in your own territory. Give yourself plenty of time to reflect, to review what you've heard, seen, and read. Share the information with your attorney, accountant, and family.

If you can afford to, take your attorney with you when you visit the franchisor's headquarters. It might also pay to hire a franchise consultant for an insider's opinion on the merits of the franchise.

Be sure you've completed your homework and know exactly what facts, if any, lie hidden behind and between the lines of the franchisor's disclosure document.

Assessing Your Franchise Buying Behavior

The following work sheet contains some important questions to help you gauge your financial, intellectual, and emotional commitments; identify potential obstacles; and define the essential benefits of a franchise opportunity.

Financial Commitment

- ☐ Overall, does the business seem worth the initial investment?

- ☐ Do you think the initial fee fairly reflects the franchisor's costs of putting you in business?

- ☐ Are you willing to pay the franchise royalty every month from your gross revenues?

- ☐ After deducting your royalty payments, will you still be able to earn a decent profit?

Rational Commitment

- ☐ What does the franchisor offer that you can't otherwise do or acquire by yourself?

- ☐ Will the value of the business appreciate over the years?

- ☐ Does the franchisor have a solid track record?

- ☐ Are other franchisees of the franchisor satisfied with their investments?

Emotional Commitment

- ☐ If you invest in the franchise, will you be proud to be its owner?

- ☐ If you have your choice of any business to enter, would you pick the one in which the franchise is engaged?

- ☐ Do you have a special interest or hobby related to the business?

- ☐ Are you excited about belonging to this field?

Obstacles and Benefits

- ☐ Is a franchise available for the location, territory, or market that you are interested in? How flexible are you about the location of the franchise?

- ☐ Will the franchise agreement allow you enough time to arrange financing and develop the business? How flexible is the franchisor about timing?

- ☐ Do you know enough about the franchise to make an informed decision? Have you checked out the franchisor's background?

- ☐ Have you been pressured to sign the franchise agreement or pay any initial fee(s) before reading the FDD and having the franchise agreement read by an attorney?

Can you handle the investment?

- ☐ Do you have sufficient credit or collateral to arrange financing?

- ☐ Will you have any partners, stockholders, or other investors?

- ☐ Is the franchisor's image conducive with that of a successful business?

- ☐ Is the franchise conducive with your own self-image and self-esteem?

9
A FRANCHISEE'S RIGHTS AND OBLIGATIONS

"In the final analysis, the one quality that all successful people have is the ability to take on responsibility."
Michael Korda

No issue in franchising is more important—or has received more publicity—than the legal, ethical, and financial relationship between franchisors and franchisees. In the 1960s and 1970s, the main problems of the industry were associated with fraud in the sale of franchises or violations of antitrust laws. The 1980s and 1990s were a period of rapid expansion of franchise outlets. That expansion, combined with the economic downturn of the latter part of the decade, caused a substantial percentage of franchisees to experience financial difficulties.

In recent years, disputes between franchisors and franchisees have received widespread publicity. Most of these disagreements focused on the mutual rights and obligations of franchisors and their franchisees.

At various times, I have been asked to testify as an expert witness in court cases involving franchise disputes. In most of these cases, the main issue was the franchisor's "duty of competence"—an implied obligation to provide know-how and support to franchisees.

What makes up a franchisor's "duty of competence?" Merely by offering a franchise, a franchisor implicitly alleges that it possesses specific knowledge and skills related to its industry. By selling a franchise, the franchisor also implies that the franchisee has the appropriate personal traits and abilities to succeed in the business. If a franchisor fails to provide adequate training or ongoing assistance, it violates its implied duty to help franchisees achieve success. However, the franchisor is not always to blame if a franchisee fails.

A franchise is not a guarantee of financial success. Frankly, some investors embark on franchising without the slightest notion of the long hours of hard work that are required to make a business profitable. Many prospective franchisees who previously held "nine-to-five" jobs are unprepared, both mentally and emotionally, for the twelve-hour work days and seven-day work weeks that lie ahead.

The International Franchise Association (IFA), which promotes the interests of franchisors, insists that reports of franchise failures and disputes are exaggerated. But the House Committee of Small Business of the U.S. Congress wants to pass new laws to regulate the relationship between franchisors and franchisees.

Various state laws already provide franchisees with special rights. For example, some states give franchisees with the right to renew their franchise agreements upon expiration and protect franchisees from involuntary termination.

Most of the franchisee's rights and obligations are defined by the franchise operating manual and in other written communications, such as newsletters and bulletins.

Obligations of a Franchisee

From a franchisor's point of view, uniform standards are key aspects of a franchise. Consumers patronize a franchise outlet because of an assurance that the level of performance, quality, and service will be largely the same from one outlet to another.

To maintain uniformity among outlets, franchisors commonly require their franchisees to adhere to strict standards and specifications. Typically, a franchisee is obligated to maintain high standards of integrity and ethical business conduct, and to promote a favorable image in all conduct with the public. Franchisees are required to maintain all licenses, permits, certificates, and other applicable documentation required by community and state laws. They must also promise to pay all fees and royalties due to their franchisor, as well as suppliers, promptly and accurately.

Franchisees are required to maintain their places of business in a clean and orderly condition, and to keep all equipment, inventory, and supplies in proper working condition. In particular, they must maintain a clean, attractive, efficient customer area, with proper safeguards and security.

A franchisee must also agree to maintain fair but rigorously enforced personnel policies to promote a favorable image to the public. They must also adhere to all franchise standards and specifications for advertising, inventory, quality, service, performance, working hours, and procedures.

Franchise Reports

Besides adhering to quality standards, franchisees are also required to furnish their franchisors with various types of reports. The following are typical:

1. Weekly Summary A summary of the outlet's sales may be required weekly.

2. Monthly Recap A recap of weekly sales may be required monthly.

3. Operating Statement (Profit and Loss Sheet) A statement of the outlet's income and expenses, showing the businesses profits or losses, may be required monthly, quarterly, or annually.

4. Proforma Operating Statement (Projected Profit and Loss Sheet) A projection of the outlet's future income and expenses, showing anticipated profits or losses, may also be required monthly, quarterly, or annually.

5. Federal Tax Return(s) Franchisees may be required to submit a true and accurate copy of their federal tax returns, or those portions relating to the franchise business, within a reasonable time after the date of filing.

6. Miscellaneous Reports In addition to those named above, franchisees may be required to submit any of the following occurrences in writing, within a specified time after the event:

Changes in ownership
If the franchise outlet is operated by a corporation, the franchisee may be required to report the names and addresses of any new shareholders, or address changes of any existing shareholders.

Changes in management
Franchisees may be required to promptly report any changes among the principal management of the franchise outlet.

Equipment failures
Franchisees may be required to promptly report breakdowns or damage to any equipment that may be required to operate the business.

Trademark infringements
The franchise agreement may obligate franchisees to assist in protecting the franchise name and trademarks, by promptly reporting any apparent infringement or unauthorized use of the trademark by another business.

Outlet Maintenance

Franchisees are usually required to maintain the condition and appearance of their franchise outlets according to exact quality standards. Franchisees are usually required to pay for all routine and normal maintenance and repair; replacement of worn-out or obsolete accessories, fixtures, equipment, signs, equipment, obsolete or unsellable inventory; and periodic refurbishing of the facilities.

Franchisors specifically prohibit their franchisees from making any material alterations to the outlet or to the business system without prior approval in writing from the franchisor. This prohibition may apply to the layout, accessories, fixtures, signs, or equipment of the outlet.

Appearance and Grooming of Employees

The franchise operating manual may include detailed standards for appearance and grooming on the job. The franchisee is responsible for assuring that employees exhibit neatness, cleanliness, and a friendly, professional demeanor toward customers.

Inspections and Audits

To assure uniform standards of image, conduct, and performance, franchisors usually reserve the right to periodically evaluate their franchisees' outlets. In personal inspections by a field manager or other representative, franchisees may be monitored for adherence to the franchisor's standards, specifications, policies, and procedures. In addition, the outlet may be subject to an unannounced audit of its books and records.

If the franchisor should discover a discrepancy in the reporting of franchise royalties or other fees, the franchisee may be held responsible for paying all costs associated with the audit.

Rights of a Franchisee

Although the franchise agreement and operating manual define many of the rights and obligations of a franchisee, various federal and state laws provide franchisees with specific rights. Many of these rights are derived from case law.

Case law is based on court decisions, in contrast to statutory laws enacted by legislative bodies. Most case law is determined by decisions rendered by federal and state appellate judges. Appellate courts (courts of appeals) are courts that hear cases that have already been decided by lower trial courts. The decisions and opinions of the appellate judges are published in documents known as "reporters."

When a case has been decided by a lower trial court, the decision may be appealed to an appellate court. For example, a case decided in a federal district court may be appealed to a federal court of appeals. The appellate court has the authority to redecide the case based on arguments presented by the opposing parties.

After both parties to the lawsuit, or litigation, have submitted briefs and presented arguments, the judge, or in some cases, a panel of judges, renders its decision to reverse or affirm the decision of the lower court. When a panel of judges votes to render a decision, the view of the judges who voted in favor of the winning decision is called the "majority opinion." Likewise, the views held by the judges who voted against the winning decision are called the "minority opinion."

The courts have helped to shape franchising practices in numerous ways. Several landmark decisions established the ground rules for price fixing, tie-in arrangements, vicarious liability, and quality standards.

Price Fixing

In *Coors Brewery v. U.S. Federal Trade Commission* and again in *U.S. v. Parke Davis & Co.*, the courts originally ruled that franchisors and other contractors may not fix the prices at which franchisees sell products to the public. Any minimum or maximum price was deemed to be an instance of illegal price fixing.

In 2010, a franchisee association sued Burger King Corporation over its decision to set a $1.00 maximum price for the "double cheeseburger," as part of a special "$1.00 Value Meal" menu. The franchisees claimed that Burger King did not have the right under its franchise agreement to unilaterally impose maximum prices to be charged by franchisees to customers.

The court ruled that the franchise agreement specifically authorized the franchisor to make changes to the operating standards and granted Burger King the discretion to set maximum prices. In reaching its conclusion, the court noted that the price being set pertained only to a single product, and that the franchisees had not proved that their entire business would suffer serious injury.

A few years later, another federal court addressed a similar issue in *Stuller, Inc. v. Steak N Shake Enterprises, Inc.* However, in this case, the franchisor attempted to set the prices the franchisees would charge for not just one item, but for virtually all the items on their menu. The court concluded that the "System" did not include pricing or promotions, and sided with the franchisees.

As these decisions demonstrate, whether a franchisor can enforce a maximum price depends on the wording of the franchise agreement, specifically with regard to the definition of the "System," as well what impact the prices have on the franchisee's business. The crux of these court rulings is that vertical price fixing, in the form of a maximum or minimum price, will generally not violate federal antitrust laws. However, it should be noted that the laws of specific states may be more strict. For example, Alabama statutes protect free trade and commerce at the state level by prohibiting unfair restraints such as price fixing and monopolies.

Tie-In Arrangements

In *Siegel v. Chicken Delight*, the Supreme Court declared that franchisors may not, without reasonable justification, force franchisees to purchase equipment and supplies from designated suppliers. But, in *Krehl v. Baskin-Robbins*, the court upheld the right Baskin-Robbins to obligate franchisees to purchase and sell only its private brand of ice cream. The distinguishing factor, said the court, is whether a product is trademarked, unique, and not generally available from other sources.

Courts have generally applied three standards to determine whether a tie-in arrangement is illegal:

(1) whether the franchisor tied together the sale of two distinct products or services

(2) whether the franchisor possesses enough economic power to coerce its customers into purchasing the tied product

(3) whether the tying arrangement affects a 'not insubstantial volume of commerce' in the tied product market

In plain language, the issue is not whether there is a tie-in arrangement, but rather whether the arrangement is justifiable. The *Siegel* court distinguished between two types of franchise systems: those set up to distribute trade-marked goods of the franchisor, and those set up "to conduct a certain business under a common trademark or trade name."

In *Principe v. McDonald's Corp.*, the court ruled that a store lease can be legally tied in with a franchise agreement. On appeal, the higher court held that there was no illegal tie-in arrangement because the lease was not separable from the franchise to which it pertained. The judge opined that "the proper inquiry is not whether the allegedly tied products are associated in the public mind with the franchisor's trademark, but whether they are integral components of the business method being franchised."

Vicarious Liability

In 1986, a Docktor Pet franchisee was sued by a customer who had bought what he thought was a purebred Doberman Pincher. The store had misrepresented the dog's authenticity, and the franchisor was held to be vicariously liable for the conduct of its franchisee.

In another landmark case involving Avis Rent A Car, an appellate court declared that the franchisor was equally liable for an accidental death caused by one of its franchisees.

Conversely, a district court in Kansas found that a gasoline franchisor was not vicariously liable for a franchisee's racial discrimination against a customer. In *Patterson v. Domino's Pizza, LLC*, the California Supreme Court similarly ruled that the franchisor was not liable for sexual harassment of a franchisee.

Quality Standards

In *Ramada Inns v. Gadsden Motel Co.*, a federal appellate judge ruled that franchisors have the right to require their franchisees to upgrade their outlets to meet new quality standards. Ramada Inns had terminated a franchisee for deficiencies under the franchise agreement and instructed the owner to cease using the franchisor's trademark. When the franchisee failed to comply, Ramada was awarded more than $250,000 in damages for injuries to its reputation.

Arbitrating Disputes

Arbitration is the resolution of a legal or contract dispute by a disinterested third party. Arbitration is an alternative to court action. Both parties in a dispute agree to be bound by the decision of an independent arbitrator.

In disputes between a franchisor and a franchisee, a third-party arbitrator, such as the American Arbitration Association, can usually render a decision much faster and at far less cost than the courts. In addition, most arbitration hearings are conducted in private, out of public view, minimizing the potential for negative publicity for either party.

Approximately one fourth of the franchise agreements currently in force include arbitration clauses stipulating that dispute between the franchisor and franchisee are to be decided by arbitration. Under such clauses, both parties agree to submit any grievances or disputes to the designated arbitrator and to be bound by whatever decision is finally rendered.

From a franchisee's standpoint, arbitration helps to assure fair practices by the franchisor. From a franchisor's perspective, an agreement to submit to arbitration helps control litigation costs and enhances the ethical image of the franchise industry.

The International Franchise Association encourages its members to use negotiation and arbitration wherever possible to resolve franchisor-franchisee disputes.

Obviously, no one—neither a franchisor nor a prospective franchisee—enters into a franchise agreement with the specific intention of violating the contract, running the outlet into the ground, and spending years in costly and time-consuming litigation. Nevertheless, as franchisors and franchisees continue to grow in number, conflict, disputes and lawsuits continue to take center stage.

Before signing a franchise agreement, it pays to clarify any representations or statements made by the franchisor. Keep detailed notes of all discussions with the franchisor. Be certain that the franchise agreement includes all the terms that have been agreed upon with the franchisor.

It is wise to obtain independent legal and accounting advice early, and to obtain an independent feasibility study or site report on the outlet premises. A prospective franchisee should conduct his or her own due diligence regarding the franchise network, by communicating with other franchisees, both existing and former.

Buyers should know their obligations under the laws that apply to the business, and not just rely on the franchisor. It is important to address any issues of concern with the franchisor early. As soon as conflicts arise, the dispute resolution processes in the franchise agreement should be invoked.

To quote the actor Graham Brown, "Life is about choices. Some we regret, some we're proud of. Some will haunt us forever. The message: we are what we chose to be."

10
WHY FRANCHISE DISPUTES HAPPEN

"No matter how thin you slice it, there will always be two sides."
Spinoza

In both theory and practice, a franchise is a breeding ground for disputes, owing to the nature of the relationship between franchisors and franchisees. Acquiring a franchise typically involves a substantial initial investment along with a continuing royalty payment. In return, the franchisee expects to obtain the benefits of a valuable trademark, the franchisor's expertise, and on-going assistance in operating the business. Franchisees also anticipate some degree of success based on the franchisor's track record.

It is worth emphasizing two basic principles at the very heart of franchising: (1) the franchisor engages in franchising to become wealthy, or, in the case of a large corporation, to increase revenues and the value of its stock, and (2) in order for these objectives to be fulfilled, the largest possible percentage of franchises sold must be successful.

Failed or lackluster franchise outlets benefit neither party. Worse, a bad franchise outcome may bring financial ruin to the franchisee and a negative reputation, as well as potentially millions in legal costs, to the franchisor. As mentioned previously, even the largest franchise corporations are vulnerable to often substantial stock losses from negative publicity about outlet closings.

When a franchise outlet fails, the franchisee's first instinct is to lay blame on the franchisor. Common complaints include lack of franchisor support, supply problems, lack of an adequate customer base, and misrepresentation of potential earnings.

Often, the parties seek a commercial solution, avoiding the costs and aggravation of litigation. However, most franchisors have a good reason to adopt a tough position; they have a real need to protect the goodwill of the franchise system. Conversely, from a franchisee's perspective, once the relationship has soured, the minimum acceptable resolution may be a parting of the ways.

Why Franchise Disputes Arise

Basically, disputes arise when a franchisee's business fails to perform to expectation, or, in the most severe cases, fails completely. They also arise when a franchisor detects that a franchisee is in violation of some aspect of the franchise agreement or has otherwise mismanaged the business. According to court records, the most common disputes involve earnings claims, the franchise's territory, contract renewal, involuntary termination, and covenants not to compete. As a dispute becomes exacerbated, the seeds for litigation are planted.

When a franchisee perceives that the business is not as successful as expected, a number of consequences may follow, such as a belief that the franchisor has failed to provide adequate assistance or that the franchisor made false earnings claims. A franchise business can also suffer losses if the territory size is inadequate, too many outlets are located in close proximity to one another, or the franchisor encroaches on the territory.

Undoubtedly, many outlets are opened with the franchisee's expectation that customers will walk through the door spontaneously, for no other reasons than the franchisor's trademark, product appeal, and advertising campaigns. Also undoubtedly, there are franchise sales representatives who encourage such an expectation, whether or not substantiated by any facts.

Disputes are inevitable if a franchisor's recruitment standards are lax or absent; for example, when a franchise is sold to anyone who wants one without regard to the applicant's managerial skills and aptitudes. A common complaint by unhappy franchisees is that the franchisor "oversold" the franchise; for example, by exaggerating its viability or minimizing its managerial and financial burdens. Quite a number of complaints are based on questionable sales tactics, such as false urgency or fictitious earnings claims.

When a franchisor has saturated the market by selling too many outlets, inevitably the performance of each franchise outlet can be expected to suffer. Franchisors that have overexpanded often are unable to provide adequate support or enforce uniform standards, creating ill will among customers as well as outlet owners.

Some franchisor have, at various times, acted unilaterally to alter specific provisions of the franchise agreement by changing some aspect of the operating standards or imposing new fees. Often, in such cases, the franchisee may perceive that the franchisor violated the franchise agreement. Part of the problem stems from the basic premise that a franchisor must treat all franchisees equally. Concessions or modifications affecting one franchisee invariably create dissention among other franchisees, who might well wonder "why am I not being treated the same?"

To be sure, there are indeed dishonest franchisors, who have little or no interest in the fate of the people who buy their franchises, or, in the worst cases, merely sell merchandise or store fixtures under the guise of a franchise operation.

Many disputes center on a franchisor terminating a franchise agreement involuntarily, usually because the franchisee stopped paying royalties, violated some aspect of the operating standards, or committed a crime. A number of franchisees have claimed that their franchises were terminated because the franchisor wanted to "seize" their outlets to resell at a profit. Similar issues may arise when a franchise agreement comes up for renewal. Typically, a franchisee has the right to renew the agreement at the end of the term, unless he or she is in violation of any provisions of the agreement. Some franchisors have been accused of inventing or exaggerating franchisee violations in order to block the contract from being renewed automatically.

From the franchisor's perspective, reselling existing outlets maximizes the profitability of the franchise. Few franchisees, however, are happy to part with ten years of dedicated hard work and financial commitment, which, from their point of view, kept the business open during that time.

The most common reason franchisors originate a dispute is that the franchisee stopped paying royalties. Usually, the franchisee did so because of an unresolved dispute, but there are cases where the outlet owner simply wanted to continue operating the business without being associated with the franchisor.

Another common area of dispute is the ability of a franchisor to enforce a noncompete provision in the franchise agreement. Many, if not most, agreements contain such a provision, prohibiting the franchisee from engaging in any business or activity in direct competition with the franchise business. However, several states have enacted laws that bar noncompete clauses from being enforced. The California Franchise Relations Act, for example, declares any such contract provision to be void.

How Franchise Disputes Arise

To say that "the best way to resolve a dispute is to avoid it" is an over-used cliché, but nevertheless accurate. It cannot be overlooked that many disputes arise because the franchisee failed to exercise due diligence before signing the agreement and paying the initial fee. Some franchisees, after opening the outlet, made poor personnel decisions or mismanaged the business. Undoubtedly, some purposefully violated the franchise agreement, though there are also cases where operating standards were violated inadvertently or without the franchisee's awareness that a violation had occurred.

Franchises have been terminated because of a smudge on a bathroom mirror or a wrinkled menu, begging the question: Did the franchisor use these seemingly minor incidents as a pretense to expunge the franchise holder from the system?

There are numerous reasons why a franchise business might fail to meet the franchisee's expectations. For one, the franchisee might have been over-extended financially, with an unreasonable debt burden and inadequate working capital. A fatal mistake is to fail to anticipate the funds that will be required to keep the business running until it begins to turn a profit. Loan payments and royalties add a burden to the outlet's operating expenses that a nonfranchise business does not have to account for.

When a franchise fails because the franchisee is unqualified for the business, both parties share the blame. The franchisee failed to exercise due diligence, whereas the franchisor failed to qualify the buyer. A number of franchise sales representatives have been accused of using persuasive sales methods to close sales regardless of the applicant's likelihood of success.

Most people normally will not invest in a franchise business without having some idea of the potential earnings and the expectation of exclusivity. If the outlet begins to fail, or the franchisee perceives that the franchisor is not providing adequate support, the franchisee will often decide to continue in the business without using the franchisor's trademark.

The single most common area of dispute in franchising involves complaints that the franchisor presented false earnings claims before the contract was signed. However, a standard clause in the Franchise Disclosure Document states that the franchisee acknowledges that he or she has not relied on any statements of projected sales or earnings, in effect negating any dispute based on earnings claims.

Clashes over territorial rights inevitably occur due to the franchisee's need for an adequate customer base and the franchisor's desire to continue to expand. Eventually, as markets become saturated, the franchisor may begin to place new outlets within close proximity to existing ones. In fact, many franchise agreements allow the franchisor to void the franchisee's exclusive territory and even compete with the franchisee within the boundaries.

To be sure, there are also dishonest franchisees who have been caught submitting false financial reports, cheating on their taxes, or hiding pertinent facts about the business from the franchisor.

It should not be overlooked that virtually every franchise is subject to shifts in the market and product demand due to changing consumer habits and public tastes. Many of the franchise outlets—and entire chains—that are currently undergoing dramatic declines in sales have fallen victim to this phenomenon.

Resolving Disputes

All disputes are eventually resolved, one way or another, via one of four vehicles:

- Workout
- Mediation
- Arbitration
- Courts of law

Workout

In all but the most flagrant instances, it behooves the parties of any franchise dispute to attempt to work out the issue through discussion and negotiation. Fittingly, franchisors refer to this process as a "workout" (no relation to physical fitness exercises).

Many franchisors use advisory councils to handle dispute resolution and attempt to devise workouts. Another option is an Ombudsman program, offering a skilled third party who works to achieve a satisfactory outcome. The largest franchise systems may employ a full-time internal ombudsman, whereas smaller systems may utilize an external ombudsman on an as-needed basis.

Mediation

Mediation is a method of trying to resolve a dispute with the assistance of an outside professional, known fittingly as the mediator. The aim is to reach a settlement as amicably as possible, with an outcome that is acceptable, if not totally agreeable, to both parties.

During mediation, each party presents its side of the dispute to the mediator, usually by giving a summary in a joint session and, then, by discussing specifics in private; i.e., without the opposing party's presence. The mediator, who is not a party to the dispute, offers suggestions as to how the issues can be resolved. Unlike a court judge, the mediator has no authority to force a solution. He or she can only assist the parties in reaching a negotiated agreement. If the dispute remains unresolved, other options, such as arbitration or a lawsuit, come into play.

The National Franchise Mediation Program (NFMP) was established in 1993 by a group of franchisors seeking a way to resolve disputes without the rancor and cost of litigation. The program is administered by the CPR Institute for

Dispute Resolution and is governed by a steering committee comprising equal numbers of franchisee and franchisor representatives. Participating franchisors agree to negotiate or, if necessary, mediate with franchisees who assert claims. Franchisee participation is voluntary.

Arbitration

Many franchise agreements now contain a clause requiring arbitration in the event of a dispute between the parties. The following verbiage suggested by the American Arbitration Association is a typical example:

> *Any controversy or claim arising out of or relating to this contract, or the breach thereof, shall be settled by arbitration administered by the American Arbitration Association in accordance with its Commercial [or other] Arbitration Rules, and judgment on the award rendered by the arbitrator(s) may be entered in any court having jurisdiction thereof.*

The clause may name a specific arbitration agency or organization to be used, as well as the state where the proceeding will take place. Additional clauses may be included regarding the number of arbitrators, the types of documents that can be submitted, and other aspects of the proceeding.

During arbitration, the parties present their cases to one or more impartial adjudicators, or arbitrators, usually attorneys or retired judges. The disputants agree to abide by the arbitrator's decision. Unless the franchise agreement includes a specific provision allowing for the arbitrator's decision to be appealed, the process stops at this point.

Courts of Law

Another hackneyed but accurate cliché about disputes is that when a case goes to trial, "nobody wins but the lawyers." A lawsuit may continue for years, even decades, and incur vast costs, as the case makes its way through the various courts of appeals. Appellate courts may disagree with lower courts, judges may overturn jury verdicts, and cases may be sent back to a lower court, starting the process all over again.

In the end, only 1.8%—less than one of every five—lawsuits result in a verdict.

Court decisions often differ on the same topic, depending on the state where the franchisee or the franchise outlet is located. Still other cases are decided based on the state where the franchisor is located or where the franchise agreement was signed.

The only thing about franchise-related litigation that can be stated with certainty is that the outcome is likely to be uncertain. For several decades, conflicting judgments have been handed down concerning such issues as territory encroachment, vicarious liability of franchisors, noncompete covenants, involuntary termination, and false earnings claims.

On the subject of juries, it should be pointed out that many franchise agreements contain a jury waiver clause. This clause provides that the parties waive their Seventh Amendment right to a trial by jury if there is any dispute arising out of or relating to the agreement. In other words, any trial will be decided by judge, not a jury.

The issue of jury waiver clauses in franchise agreements was examined in 1999 in a suit against a franchisor for "fraudulent nondisclosure and fraudulent inducement." The franchisee's attorney claimed that because the franchisee was fraudulently induced into entering into the franchise agreement, the jury waiver clause was unenforceable.

In its ruling, the court left open the possibility that there may be instances where a jury waiver clause is void if the contract was fraudulently induced. With that principle in mind, the court outlined four factors for determining the validity of a jury waiver clause: (1) the relative bargaining powers of the parties, (2) the franchisee's understanding of the provisions, (3) whether the waiver was negotiated, and (4) whether the provision was conspicuous.

The fact is that the true objective of most civil litigation today is not winning at trial, but optimizing bargaining leverage in an eventual settlement. On the rare occasion when parties invoke their constitutional right to try a case to its conclusion, many judges would opine that "someone is being unreasonable."

Anatomy of an Arbitration

Though arbitration proceedings may be subject to procedures established by different state laws, the following processes are typical. Unlike court litigation, arbitration proceedings are normally conducted in private.

Written submissions

The parties to the dispute will be asked to submit written descriptions of their argument before meeting with the arbitrator or tribunal. The parties may expand on their legal arguments in further written submissions, or "memorials," including statements from witnesses, expert opinions, and pertinent documents. A second round of submissions may take place, to give the parties an opportunity to reply.

Document production

Generally, the parties to an arbitration are only required to produce documents that support their case. Document production is an important stage of the process. The outcome of any dispute will be determined based on the specific facts of the case; documents are almost always more persuasive than an individual's oral testimony.

Oral hearing

Once the disputants' pleadings, evidence and disclosure have been submitted, there is often an evidential hearing—an oral hearing involving all parties to the dispute. The evidential hearing provides each disputant with the opportunity to explain their case to the arbitrator, answer any questions that arise, and to challenge and discredit evidence presented by the opposing party. Opening statements may be limited to specific points raised by the arbitrator, followed by witness testimony and expert opinions. As in a court case, questions may be posed by the opposing party's attorney or advocate, as well as by the arbitrator.

Post-hearing submissions

Post-hearing written submissions are usually provided shortly after the hearing has finished. The arbitrator usually requests that the parties review and correct the transcript and submit additional documents pertinent to the amount of any award. The arbitrator may also request briefs relating to specific questions or issues.

Decision and Award

Following this process, the arbitrator may declare the proceedings closed. At this point, the parties have are no longer entitled to submit further evidence or arguments. The arbitrator then proceeds to publish its decision. The outcome is considered final and not subject to appeal (unless the parties previously agreed otherwise).

11
FRANCHISING AND TECHNOLOGY

"The problem is not whether machines think, but whether men do."
B. F. Skinner

Over the last 20 years, technology has dramatically transformed social behavior, education, and health care, not only in the United States but across the globe. Nowhere is the impact of technology and innovation felt more profoundly than in franchising and retailing. For a franchisor, internet marketing, data mining, and social media have become essential tools for growth.

Social media websites provide a delivery vehicle for the organization's sales messages, but also a stage for consumer reaction and reviews. Comments posted by customers on Facebook, Twitter, Pinterest, Reddit, or LinkedIn have the power to drastically boost or sabotage sales. News reports of negative incidents have caused the sales of entire franchise chains to plummet, resulting in losses in the millions.

The Rise of Artificial Intelligence

Social media aside, arguably the most important influence of advancing technology on franchising is Artificial Intelligence (AI). In the popular imagination, AI is often envisioned as the proliferation of self-aware robots, but in fact, machine intelligence is more commonly implemented to accomplish a wide range of relatively mundane tasks. Few of us yet interact with robots or ride in self-controlled drones, but our daily lives are increasingly affected by AI systems that can recognize speech or images, or analyze patterns of online behavior.

Since the 1960s, AI has been used to mine for profits, streamline business environments, and cultivate customer buying behavior. As of this writing, AI is present in almost all forms of enterprise, from banks, health care providers, and insurance companies to manufacturers, utility companies, and website marketers. In the corporate workplace, AI is widely used for complex problem solving and decision support in disciplines ranging from financial management to forecasting. It is a characteristic of modern economies that data increases exponentially literally day by day. Analyzing this growing body of information and formulating quick and accurate decisions requires complex cognitive abilities available only to machine intelligence.

From the moment the alarm clock wakens us each morning to the moment we turn out the light on the nightstand, AI already affects us more than any scientific or cultural phenomenon has influenced people at any previous time in history (other than the threat of nuclear war). As the future unfolds, the impact of AI on the personal life, work, leisure time, and health of every individual in the workplace will continue to multiply.

This event will occur gradually, not with some sudden overnight revelation; yet, inexorably intelligent machines will become indispensable to the existence of virtually everyone on the planet. Most people will accept the consequences as a normal—and perhaps necessary—aspect of their daily lives.

Today, the toothpaste we use, the clothing we put on, the vehicles we drive, the tools we use, the grocery items we purchase, our entertainment choices, and even our romantic prospects, are designed, engineered, produced, marketed, inventoried, or referred to us as a result of AI technology. In the future, it may not even be necessary to drive one's own car to work—or even, for that matter, to show up for work at all.

Technological advancements have already obsoleted workers in a number of fields. This trend inexorably will increase with the introduction of more machines that are more intelligent. New entrants into the workforce will require training to program, maintain, and work with intelligent machines. Nevertheless, the fear of technology-related job loss concentrated at the lower end of the income scale is very real. As the AI boom continues, there is every likelihood that not only white-collar workers but also executives at all levels of management will be affected by the proliferation of intelligent machines.

One reason for the AI boom is the analytical power made possible by artificial neural networks (ANNs) patterned after the human brain. In some applications, such as fraud detection and credit card processing, AI has already become the technology of preference. In addition, the use of neural networks has become an established methodology for pattern recognition, particularly of images, data streams and complex data sources. Such networks have emerged as the platform for the majority of data-mining tools currently in use.

Besides fraud detection, AI is used to analyze and manage the buying habits of consumers, as well as manage production and delivery schedules based on customer demand. By eliminating downtime due to unpredictable scheduling, such systems increase productivity and profits.

With the rise of online purchasing and social media, AI began to be applied to collecting, processing, and analyzing information on a massive scale, giving rise to the pop-science terms Big Data, analytics, and data mining.

Franchising and Big Data

Big Data, in a general sense, refers to a very large and rapidly growing volume of information, beyond the ability of conventional computer technology to process efficiently. In a typical enterprise environment, the information results from Internet usage, social media, and computing task such as word processing or accounting. However, if you ask ten professionals in computer-related fields to define Big Data, the chances are that you will receive at least seven different definitions.

To a franchise chain, Big Data is composed of all the information collected from every customer, as well as the results of analyzing that information. To a physicist, Big Data consists of all the information generated by humans, the media, and computers. Virtually every entity that has a reason to use the buzzword in its literature and media has its own "take" slanted toward its own interests. Regardless of the slant, analytics and data mining are integral to harnessing and harvesting it.

In logic, analytics refers to the logical science of analysis. In data mining, analytics involves the entire process of collecting, analyzing, and drawing conclusions from a growing body of data. From a business perspective, analytics enables management to view, at any point in time, how customers or users utilize a product or service, as well as demographic and behavioral traits, such as age, gender, buying habits, personal interests, and so forth.

Data mining gives the franchisors who use it a precise view of how particular segments of the customer base react to a product or service, and proposes changes consistent with those findings. In addition to exploring customers' buying patterns, analytics enables management to react much more quickly to marketplace changes. The results enable a franchisor to refresh marketing models on the fly, based on each new incoming piece of customer information, to create a more targeted offering.

Data mining techniques are largely identical to those used by computer viruses. In fact, programs that infect computers with programs designed to provide feedback about the internet browsing habits of users are classified as malware in many antivirus databases, as are programs designed to deliver targeted advertisements.

Like a virus, a data mining program secretly intrudes on a user's computer without permission. The program seeks out specific locations on the computer, such as email folders and places where downloads and preferences are stored, and then harvests pertinent data about the user. The program's instructions are in the form of "scripts" that waken automatically when a user accesses the web page to which they are attached.

Data mining scripts are now present on most e-commerce web pages, as well as the sites of many governments and institutions. The information they extract from users' computers is used to create custom product offerings, compile demographic data, and guard against fraud, but also to generate email lists for target marketing ("spam").

Most merchandising websites track customer purchases so that the most relevant products can be displayed each time the user accesses the site. Consumers' buying habits are often sold to other marketers for use in email campaigns or pop-up ads.

Merely reaping information and storing it in a big database are, by themselves, of minimal use. To be meaningful, well as profitable, the mined data must be sorted into identifiable patterns and relationships, or behaviors. Once these behaviors are defined, they then need to be validated.

The resulting information can be used to predict future behaviors, such as purchasing similar or related products. The data can also reveal personal traits, such as age, gender, occupation, hobbies, entertainment preferences, and health status. For example, analytics would predict that a computer user who browses for women's hair coloring and anti-wrinkle cream is most likely a female 40 years or older. Based on statistics about 40-year-old females, the program might predict that the user would also be interested in a certain style of apparel.

Left to its own devices, a data mining system may develop subtle patterns that might otherwise evade normal expectations. A classic case is a supermarket that prominently juxtaposed displays of beer and diapers, creating a seemingly humorous correlation between alcohol consumption and urinary urgency. The displays were actually based on predictive modeling derived from data mining. According to the analytics, males who are fathers of infants and happen to do the grocery shopping on Saturday tend to buy both beer and diapers. The predictive model was validated by a surge in sales of both items.

The focus of data mining systems is on defining behaviors that are useful in generating reliable predictions. Web tracking—identifying and correlating websites visited by a single user—has become a common instrument for mining data about internet users. In an experiment performed by researchers at Princeton University, Google Analytics web tracking scripts were found on more than 70 percent of the websites they studied. DoubleClick, an ad-serving system also developed by Google, was found on half of the sites. The researchers used software that was also developed at Princeton, to survey one million sites, logging any tracking technology that was detected.

When embedded on a large number of sites, web tracking scripts can compile detailed profiles of individual users navigating the internet. Among the documents leaked by former U.S. Department of Defense contractor Edward Snowden was a memo indicating that the National Security Agency tapped into Google's web tracking system to identify potential suspects for surveillance.

In theory, data mining techniques are based on predictive analysis using behavioral modeling and statistics. However, methods such as Google's ad-serving technique actually have built-in biases. Advertisers choose the types of users to target. To streamline the validation process, businesses often rely on heuristic shortcuts; for example, a male who browses female swimsuit photos might be presented, without any statistical basis, with an ad for an erectile dysfunction aid.

Predictably, the practice of data mining has led to controversy over privacy and ethical concerns. Nevertheless, it is an important competitive tool of the savvy franchisor.

Anyone contemplating a franchise investment should pay particular attention to the franchisor's use of technology. Without systems in place using Artificial Intelligence, data mining, and analytics, a franchisor risks becoming obsolete in the marketplace, but, more importantly, lacks the ability to deliver customers to the franchisee's doorstep in the digital era in which we live today.

Technology is also used increasingly to source, recruit, manage, and develop franchisees. A computer-assisted recruiting system captures the behavioral attributes of candidates and compares them to the technical and social requirements of the business. Machine learning techniques enable the department to track successful candidates as they operate their franchises, identifying personality traits and skills that relate to success. Analytics is used to form judgments about the appointment of franchisees, evaluate performance, and provide decision support for future recruitment efforts.

Cybercrime and Security

Unfortunately, the unavoidable offspring of data collection and point-of-sale (POS) technology is cybercrime and fraud. Whether they realize it or not, by engaging in collecting and storing personal information, franchisors are also in the data privacy and security business. The personal information obtained from consumers and social media websites has become essential to cultivating markets and recruiting future and repeat customers. The failure to protect this information is potentially disastrous.

From March, 2015 through June, 2016, an ongoing data breach occurred at Hyatt, Marriott, Sheraton, and Westin hotels in ten states and Washington, D.C, following a series of data thefts in the preceding months at Hilton, Starwood, and Omni hotels.

In 2012, a leading credit card processor, Global Payments, reported that 1.5 million credit card accounts had been compromised in a security breach. That same year, the FTC filed an action against the Wyndham Worldwide chain for failing to maintain reasonable data security, thus allowing intruders to obtain access to the computer networks of the franchisor and several franchised hotels over a two-year period. The data breaches led to the theft of 600,000 credit card accounts and fraudulent charges of more than $10.6 million.

The Wyndham case is noteworthy because it involves an important aspect of the franchise relationship: the franchisor's significant assistance and control. The franchise agreements required Wyndham hotel franchisees to "purchase and configure to their specifications, a designated computer system, known as a property management system" linked to the franchisor's computer network. The franchisor set the rules, including all password requirements, for employee access. The FTC held that that Wyndham's privacy policy misrepresented the security measures of the company and its subsidiaries and, thus, was liable for fraud under FTC regulations. Besides storing credit card data in plain text, the hotel chain failed to use firewalls, fix known security vulnerabilities, and require strong user passwords.

When a security breach occurs, federal and state regulators investigate not only the franchisor's policies and procedures, but also representations about how customer data is collected, used, and safeguarded.

Training and Development

According to the American Society for Training and Development (ASTD), annual spending by corporations on employee training represents about two percent of total payroll dollars. Increasingly, management looks to intelligent training systems to increase effectiveness, efficiency and overall return on investment. Intelligent Tutoring Systems (ITS) technology used in training rooms is capable of creating not just trained novices, but content experts. These systems provide individualized coaching, performance assessment, and feedback—activities needed for employees to acquire broad and deep expertise.

Computer-based simulations let trainees "learn by doing," replicating on-the-job situations. Pioneered by the aviation industry and the military, simulations are being adopted by more and more businesses to help trainees learn diverse subjects such as equipment and software operations and maintenance, business and analytical skills, and inter-personal skills. An essential feature of a robust simulation environment is the use of intelligent tutoring to provide coaching during exercises, assess the trainee's performance, and produce meaningful feedback. In this setting, AI training technologies have been shown to be very effective.

An ITS system assesses each learner's actions within the interactive environment and develops a model of his or her knowledge, skills, and learning pace. Instructional strategies are then tailored based on the learner model. Research using intelligent tutoring in industrial settings indicates that employees generally learn more quickly and exhibit improved job performance.

Robots in the Workplace

Developments in computer image recognition are radically transforming the workplace. Using fuzzy logic, computers can recognize objects, such as furniture and products, as well as animals, and within a few years will be able to distinguish and identify individuals. Security systems will benefit from the ability of video surveillance to distinguish people with authorized access to a building or office, from those without authorization.

With computer vision and improved language processing ability, machines will be able to identify items and better know how to interact with them. Self-driving vehicles are an example. Image recognition in health care environments will enable machines to interpret and analyze X-ray and MRI images. Humanoid robots with deep learning capability are already being deployed as virtual office receptionists, assembly line workers, and companions for the elderly or debilitated.

People and robots already work side by side in some workplaces, including manufacturing, health care, and research environments. Industrial robots are true marvels of engineering and an indispensable part of today's large manufacturing processes. Intelligent robots have taken over many of the tasks in factory operations requiring high degrees of precision, speed, and endurance. In recent years, industrial robots have become increasingly smarter, more flexible, and more autonomous, with the capacity to make decisions and work independently of humans.

Robots are expected to replace two thirds of all fast food workers within the next 30 years. According to a study by the World Economic Forum (WEF), by 2020 about seven million jobs will be lost, but only two million new jobs gained, as a result of technological change in fifteen major developed and emerging economies. Women, according to the report, will be the biggest victims. While men will see approximately one job gained for every three lost, women face more than five jobs lost for every one gained.

It is certain that technology will continue to develop rapidly, transforming not only how franchisors attract, recruit, and train franchisees, but also the very fabric of the franchise business itself.

Occupations Most at Risk of Automation

Job Title	%
Loan officers	98
Receptionists and clerks	96
Legal assistants	94
Retail sales	92
Taxi drivers/chauffeurs	89
Security guards	84
Food and Beverage Servers	77
Financial advisers	58
Newspaper reporters	11
Musicians	7
Attorneys	3

(Source: Oxford University)

12
EVALUATING FRANCHISE OFFERINGS

"It has long been an axiom of mine that the little things are infinitely the most important."
Arthur Conan Doyle

The decision whether or not to invest in a franchise—and which franchise to purchase—may well be one of the most important decisions a prospective franchisee will ever make. It would be wise not to take this decision lightly.

Behind the glossy color photographs, the meticulously groomed flagship, and the affable smile of the franchisor's representative are signposts from the past revealing details about the future. Just as a franchisor evaluates the qualifications of prospective franchisees, franchisors can also be evaluated based on their qualifications.

Following are some of the important traits for evaluation:

Length of time in business

The longer a franchisor has been in business, the more experience there is to share with franchisees. The franchising company knows what works in its line of business, but "negative" experience is equally important. Established chains know what not to do to be successful--how to avoid the innumerable mistakes, large and small, that characterize a small business when it first starts out.

Length of time in franchising

The longer a chain has been involved in franchising, the more capable it is to lead, guide, and motivate franchisees. The experienced franchisor knows what makes franchisees "tick"—their ambitions, drives, hopes, and dreams. He also knows how to handle problems and stave off crises.

Prior litigation or other legal problems

The fewer lawsuits and legal entanglements a franchisor has had, the more ethical he is likely to be, Favor the franchisor who conscientiously walks the "straight and narrow."

A history of civil action involving franchise law is a red flag for operators sometimes forming part of a lifelong behavior pattern. Some disputes and litigation may be expected, owing to the nature of the franchisor-franchisee relationship. However, among other things, legal fees burden the entire franchise organization, eating up funds that might otherwise be spent for the benefit of franchisees.

Civil actions or expulsions from securities associations

A history of civil actions involving fraud or the violation of a franchise law is a potential red flag for concern. A slogan heard too often in franchise circles is "anything's legal if you get away with it." Don't take chances.

There are some who would opine that someone who has the poor sense to buy a franchise from a convicted felon, or from someone who was once expelled from a securities association, possibly deserves whatever unsavory consequences may ensue.

Length of time in the industry

Some franchisors have spent a great deal of time in business, but a relatively small portion of this time in their current industry. For instance, a franchisor in the electronics industry sold insurance for ten years—twice as long as he has been involved with electronics. Real know-how is derived from real experience. One should give added weight to franchisors who were successful in their own industries before they launched a franchise program.

Past financial stability

A company that has maintained an even keel through times of economic hardship has extra know-how that may help you survive, as well. One should give preference to a franchisor whose company has led a life of economic stability, without undergoing numerous reorganizations, mergers, and acquisitions.

Cash reserves for handling a crisis

Study the franchisor's audited financial statement. How much cash does he have on hand? If the amount is not impressive, how many of his assets are convertible—i.e., can be easily liquidated in a crisis? One should give added weight to a franchisor who is prepared to handle cash emergencies if the economy or industry takes an unexpected turn for the worse.

Quality of training program

Ask the franchisor for an outline of the franchise training curriculum. Does it touch all the bases? Does it have real substance and value? Think of your initial fee as your tuition to attend the franchise training school, and consider whether the curriculum is worth the price.

Franchise operating manual

Ask to see the operating manual, or, if the franchisor considers it "too secret" to let you browse through, ask to inspect the table of contents. Is the manual comprehensive? Does it provide a complete how-to "bible" for planning, opening, and managing the business?

Finding the Answers

Many of the important considerations in evaluating a franchise opportunity are addressed in the Franchise Disclosure Document (FDD). However, other factors that are not required to be disclosed should also be considered. Some of these issues require independent research, personal self-evaluation, and, in some cases, best-guess judgments. In a general sense, the criteria can be categorized as follows:

- The Industry and Market
- The Company
- The Investment
- The Financial Arrangement
- Training and Support
- The Territory
- Restrictions
- Exit Strategy

The Industry and Market

Where franchising is concerned, reading the future is often as important as interpreting the past. Of course, if it is far easier to reflect on what has already occurred than to predict what will happen next. Nevertheless, no one considering a franchise investment can afford to ignore the combined influence of social, economic, and cultural trends on the business. For example, as of this writing, many retail chains are suffering significant sales declines as a result of competition from e-commerce sales by online sellers.

Clearly, there is a downside to stores failing to adapt to the consumer's changing online shopping behavior. Some franchisors even compete directly with their own franchisees through internet stores. As sales shift to the Internet, traditional brick-and-mortar retailers are closing more stores, resulting in a net decline in employment.

Commercial real estate prices are also affected by retail store closures. Shifts in consumer preferences and buying habits are significant problems for specialty franchise chains, as illustrated by the rapid decline of video rental outlets and toy stores.

Are the franchisor's industry and market rising, declining, or remaining static?

What are the demographics of the business? Does the business sell most of its products to a specific age group, or to customers in a certain income range or level of education?

Are these customer groups increasing or declining in numbers?

Is the industry well established, or based on a relatively new concept or trend?

What is the future outlook for the industry and market?

Does the franchisor use advanced technology to recruit customers to franchise outlets?

The Company

Is the franchising company a corporation whose shares traded on the stock exchange?

If so, over the last ten years has the stock increased in value, declined, or remained about the same? What is the opinion of stock brokers and investment advisers regarding the company's shares?

How long has the franchisor operated a business similar to the proposed franchise outlet? What happened to the "predecessor" businesses? Did the franchisor sell them? If so, to whom?

The disclosure document reveals the identity and experience of the principals for the last five years. What are their business backgrounds prior to five years ago? Are the disclosures current and accurate? Are there any major omissions or misrepresentations?

Have any of the principals been involved in a bankruptcy that, for some reason, may have been omitted from the disclosure document? If so, what are the particulars? Does the business in question have any bearing on the proposed franchise?

The names and addresses of established franchisees must be disclosed in the disclosure document. Is the list current and accurate?

Did you contact any existing franchisees? If so, were they satisfied with their investments? Do any of the franchisees on the list receive a fee or other consideration for endorsing the franchise operation or otherwise aiding the franchisor to sell new franchises?

Are the franchisor's audited financial statements current, within the last six months? What proportion of the franchisor's assets is represented by cash? Are any of the assets intangible?

Are the franchisor's so-called trade secrets protected by patents or copyrights?

What steps has the franchisor taken to protect the use of the franchise logo or other trademark?

Is the logo or trade mark registered with the federal government? Or is it merely registered with some local city, county, or state agency?

Has the registration been granted, or is it still "applied for?"

Are there any pending conflicts or disputes that might affect your right to use the franchise name, logo, or trade mark in your trading area?

Is a well-known public figure a prominent factor in the likelihood of your success?

Is the public figure a principal in the business, or tied to a long-term contract?

If the public figure should back out of the franchise organization, how will it affect your business? Is the main value of the franchise derived from the figure's presence or reputation?

Exactly how does the public figure benefit from his or her association with the franchise company?

Did you contact any existing franchisees? If so, were they satisfied with their investments? Do any of the franchisees on the list receive a fee or other consideration for endorsing the franchise operation or otherwise aiding the franchisor to sell new franchises?

Are the franchisor's audited financial statements current, within the last six months? What proportion of the franchisor's assets is represented by cash? Are any of the assets intangible?

How many franchisee outlets have gone out of business, declared bankruptcy, or been resold? Have more outlets opened than closed?

The Investment

What is the total amount of all fees, charges, and initial purchases payable to the franchisor? What expense items are payable as a lump sum? What items may be paid for as they are incurred? To whom must they be paid?

What is your estimated investment in leases or real estate? In equipment, fixtures, and improvements? In opening inventory purchases? In deposits?

Does the franchisor offer any financial assistance? If so, how much of your investment will he finance? At what interest rate?

Can you handle the investment, including the working capital required to sustain the business until it begins to turn a profit?

Is the franchise fee payable in a lump sum, or may it be paid in installments? Where will the initial fee be deposited: in an impoundment or escrow account, or in the "general funds" of the franchise company? Will you be entitled to a refund if, for some reason, you are unable to open the franchise? If so, how much will be refunded?

If the franchisor makes any statement regarding projected earnings of the proposed business, how were the projections calculated?

How many outlets were used by the franchisor to produce the projections? Where are they located? How long have they been in business? How long did it take them to begin yielding the sales or earnings used in the projections?

Are the projections based on average sales or earnings of actual outlets, or are they largely hypothetical; e.g., based on a predicted "trend" or average increase in sales?

Has the franchisor advised you that there is no assurance that you can actually attain the sales or earnings levels disclosed in the disclosure document?

Does the franchisor charge for site selection assistance? If so, how much is the charge and when must it be paid?

Are there any other fees, charges, or royalties besides the franchise royalty? If so, what are they, and how are they payable?

Does the franchisor charge for marketing consultation or other special assistance? If so, what is the rate and how is it incurred?

Is there a charge for the training program? If so, how much is it? Will you have to pay for your own travel and living expenses to attend the program?

Are you required to purchase an opening inventory from the franchisor or from a designated supplier? If so, what is the wholesale value?

The Financial Arrangement

Is the franchise fee payable in a lump sum, or may it be paid in installments? Where will the initial fee be deposited? In an impoundment or escrow account, or in the "general funds" of the franchise company?

Will you be entitled to a refund if, for some reason, you are unable to open the franchise? If so, how much will be refunded?

Will the franchisor have the right to terminate the agreement against your will? If so, on what grounds? Are the stated grounds legal, justifiable, or reasonable?

How does the royalty fee compare with other franchises in the same industry or market?

Does the franchisor charge an advertising fee? If so, does the franchisor have the right to raise the fee at some time in the future?

Training and Support

Specifically what services does the franchisor promise to provide as a normal part of the franchise arrangement; i.e., without additional charge?

What services will be provided prior to opening the business? Site selection assistance? Help with negotiating the lease? Help with designing and procuring signage?

What services will be provided after the business is open? Marketing assistance? Accounting help or advice? Purchasing assistance?

Does the franchisor provide a substantial training program? If so, is there an additional charge for the training, or is the cost included in the initial fee?

Have you seen a copy of the franchise operating manual? Is it comprehensive and detailed enough to serve as a blueprint for opening and running the business on a day-to-day basis?

As a rule of thumb, the ideal support ratio is one franchise representative for every 12 franchisees. Is the franchisor's ratio higher, lower, or about the same?

If you communicated with existing franchisees, how pleased are they with the franchisor's support?

Has the franchisor been involved in any disputes with current or former franchisees? If so, how were they resolved?

The Territory

Will you receive a protected territory?

Will the franchisor be allowed to sell other franchises or market products within your territory?

How is the territory defined? Are the geographic boundaries spelled out in detail?

Does the franchisor have the right to modify the territory in the future?

What is the value of the territory in terms of potential customers? Will that value be impacted if the franchisor establishes other franchises near your outlet?

Restrictions

Will you be obligated to purchase any equipment, supplies, fixtures, or inventory items from a designated supplier? If so, for what reason? Are the prices offered by a designated supplier comparable or lower than those offered by any other supplier carrying the same or comparable goods?

Will you be obligated to purchase equipment, supplies, fixtures, or inventory based on minimum technical specifications defined by the franchisor? If so, are the specifications reasonable?

Are the specifications written in such a manner as to include a number of alternative brands or makes available from a wide range of suppliers? Or are they written so as to limit the type and source?

Do you have the right to hire someone else to actively manage the business? Are you contemplating a partnership? If so, does your partner meet all the franchisor's qualifications?

What kinds of business activities, if any, are prohibited by the franchisor? Are the prohibitions reasonable?

Will you be allowed to own, operate, or participate as an investor in any other type of business besides the franchise? Will you have to sell or discontinue any other businesses you currently own?
Will entering into the franchise agreement bar you from owning stock in any particular corporation of your choosing?

Will you have to sell any stock that you currently own? On what grounds will you be able to cancel or terminate the agreement?

Are there restrictions governing your right to sell or otherwise assign the franchise to someone else? If so, are the restrictions legal and reasonable?

Exit Strategy

Will you have the right to resell the franchise to someone else? If so, under what conditions? Will the franchisor have the right of first refusal?

What will happen to the franchise if you should become disabled?

If you should die during the term of the franchise, will your heirs inherit any rights or interests in the business?

Will you lose the franchise if you should be forced to file for bankruptcy?

Franchisor Viability Index

Rate each factor on a scale of one to ten. Multiply the rating by the weight to determine the index for that factor.

Factor	Weight	Rating	Index
Company Background			
Length of time in business	.08	___	___
Length of time in franchising	.05	___	___
Litigation	.05	___	___
Civil actions	.05	___	___
Marketing Effectiveness			
Length of time in the industry	.05	___	___
Staff credentials	.05	___	___
Market share	.05	___	___
Advertising reach	.05	___	___
Number of outlets	.05	___	___
Financial Strength			
Net worth	.10	___	___
Past stability	.05	___	___
Cash reserves	.05	___	___
Franchisee Operations			
Training program	.06	___	___
Operations manual	.05	___	___
Franchisee satisfaction	.06	___	___
Industry/market strength	.15	___	___
Total			___

Use the total score to assess the overall viability of a franchise offering and to compare competing offerings. The higher the score, the more viable the franchise.

13
INSIDE THE FRANCHISE AGREEMENT

"Unless both sides win, no agreement can be permanent."
James Earl Carter, Jr.

A franchisor's attorneys are experts in drafting franchise agreements, most of which are designed to produce maximum leverage for the franchisor. Knowing how a franchise contract is drafted and what ramifications may result from each provision is one of the most valuable assets you can bring to the bargaining table.

There are almost as many different franchise agreements as there are franchise businesses, but there are many elements common to all good franchise contracts. The basic agreement has fifteen parts. Each defines one of the important relationships between franchisor and franchisee.

1. *Grant of Franchise*

You might find this part of the contract in the "preambles." The preamble section summarizes the reason for the contract and states the mutual objectives of the parties signing it. However, it may also contain some legal language that may have an enormous bearing on your rights as a franchisee.

For example, the contract may contain a statement that you have read the Franchise Disclosure Document and franchise agreement in their entirety, and accept all the terms, provisions, and covenants as being "reasonable and necessary." If you were the franchisor, you would certainly want this acknowledgment clearly stated and agreed to in writing. A franchisee involved in a legal dispute often claims that the franchisor failed to adequately explain all the details of the franchise contract. But as a prospective franchisee, be sure you really have read every word of the agreement, and understand what each sentence means.

When you sign the franchise agreement, you may also be signing an oath that could let your franchisor off the hook in the event of a future dispute over some aspect of the agreement.

The grant of franchise may also include a precisely defined territory. For example, the contract might state, "Franchisor agrees that it will not compete with Franchisee in the designated territory, nor establish another franchise therein."

In other words, the franchisor will not sell products to customers in your territory, or sell a franchise to someone else inside your territory. If a franchisor grants you a protected territory, he cannot restrain you from selling to customers outside its boundaries. The territory constrains the franchisor, not the franchisee.

2. *Trademarks and Identity*

This section of the agreement states who owns the trade name, trademarks, and logos associated with the franchise, and gives you a license to use them. The owner is usually the franchisor himself, or, possibly, a public figure affiliated with the franchisor. The agreement also obligates you to protect the franchisor's trademarks against infringement by others. In addition, you agree to use the trademarks only in a manner approved by the franchisor.

In plain English, that means the franchisor controls the business name and logo. For instance, he may let you order pens with the business name imprinted on the side, but he might want to forbid you from printing up girlie calendars featuring the company logo.

If you come across any unauthorized use of the trademarks by someone else, you are bound to notify the franchisor at once. For example, let's say you buy a franchise which uses the trade name "Supertech." One day, you come across a competitor using the name "Super Tek." It's your duty to call the franchisor and report this obvious infringement. A registered trademark has no value unless its exclusivity is protected by those who are licensed to use it.

The agreement also usually obligates you to discontinue using the franchise trademarks if the franchisor loses his own rights to them.

Simply acquiring the rights to a trademark through a franchise agreement may not give you the right to use it in your area. A franchisor secures federal registration of a trade name or mark by being the first one to implement it in interstate commerce. But someone else might already have the right to use the same name or trademark in a city, county, or state where the franchisor has not previously done business. As a result, you could actually end up buying a franchise and not being able to use the franchise name in your area.

Even though you obtain a license to use the franchisor's trademarks, you must obtain a business name permit (often called a DBA, for "doing business as") before you can use the name in your own business. A state, county, or city agency is usually responsible for dispensing these permits. The idea is to assure that competing businesses don't use the same name in the same trading area. If someone else has already acquired a permit to use the same or a similar name as your franchise, the trademark license may be a hollow commodity. Thus, investigate your right to use the franchise trademarks in your area *before* you sign the franchise agreement.

Assume, for example, that you buy a franchise which uses the trade name "Rocket Messenger." When you go to City Hall to take out a business name permit, you discover to your chagrin that another company in town already has the rights to that name. As a result, the permit is denied. Unfortunately, your franchisor's co-op advertising will be of very little value to you if you can't use the advertised name. You might be able to convince the other business to change its name, but not without compensation.

3. *Relationships of the Parties*

A franchisee is an independent business owner who contracts with a franchisor for the services and benefits specified in the agreement. As such, neither party may incur debts on the other's behalf. The franchise agreement does not make either party a subsidiary or affiliate of the other. Each is liable for his own taxes, debts, and contracts.

In plain English, your franchisor is not liable for your behavior. For example, if a customer trips on a freshly waxed floor and cracks a vertebra, you—not your franchisor—will be held liable. Likewise, if you cheat on your tax returns, it's your problem, not your franchisor's.

4. *Fees and Payments*

In this section, you agree to pay the initial franchise fee. The fee may be due on signing the agreement, or it may be payable in installments. As a franchisee, you also agree to pay the specified royalty, and to make sure it is paid on time each month. If your royalty payments are late, the agreement may stipulate interest or penalties.

If your franchisor has a co-op advertising fund, your monthly advertising royalty should also be stated in this section of the agreement.

If your franchisor will also be one of your vendors, e. g., a product distributor or equipment supplier, the agreement may give the franchisor the right to apply your royalty payments against any other amounts you may owe. For example, the contract may state something like, "Franchisor shall have sole discretion to apply any payments by

Franchisor to any past-due indebtedness of Franchisee to Franchisor. "

Let's say you buy a franchise to open a restaurant, and your franchisor happens to sell restaurant fixtures and supplies. Assume you buy these items from the franchisor on credit. Later on, when your restaurant opens, you mail in your first royalty check. To your consternation, the franchisor applies the royalty payment against the amount you owe for fixtures and supplies. As a result, your royalty remains unpaid and begins to accrue penalties.

If a provision like this appears in a franchise agreement, be sure your franchisor gives you a full and clear explanation before you sign. Ask for examples of how the provision might apply in your case.

5. *Training and Guidance*

In most franchise agreements, the franchisor agrees to provide a training program of a set length, e.g., two weeks. The agreement may require you to pay for your own travel and living costs to attend the training program. In addition, there may be a surcharge for additional attendees, such as a partner or manager. If these points are unclear in the agreement, ask the franchisor to clarify them.

The franchisor may also agree to provide other guidance and services, such as ongoing advice and consultation, a franchise manual, or assistance in selecting a site for your business.

Most franchise agreements state that the operating manual is loaned, not given or sold, to the franchisee. The logic is that the manual contains the franchisor's success secrets and, therefore, is accessible to you only during the term of your franchise. When your franchise expires, so does your access to the trade secrets. Hence, you usually must agree to return the manual and all updates, bulletins, and revisions to the franchisor if and when you and your franchisor part ways.

6. Operating System

In this section, you agree to abide by the franchisor's operating policies and performance standards. The agreement may also obligate you to help keep them secret. You might also find one or more of the following provisions:

> As a franchisee, you will be prevented from using the franchise business system in any other business.

> You must keep every aspect of the business secret. Neither you nor your employees may copy the franchise manual or any other written communication from the company.

> Employees of your franchise must sign oaths of confidentiality.

In other words, you can't buy the franchise, learn all its success secrets, and then sell those secrets to someone else. Nor can you start another business under a different name using the methods and techniques you learned from the franchisor.

These are reasonable precautions designed to protect the value of the franchise. They work in your favor, as well as your franchisor's. Your franchisor's secrets, methods, and techniques are your competitive edge; the moment they fail to remain secret, your franchise instantly loses value.

7. Development and Improvement

The franchise agreement usually requires you to lease and develop your outlet within a specified period, e.g., ninety days. You also agree to purchase the equipment, fixtures, signs, and inventory you need to open the business. The franchisor may agree to help out with Grand Opening activities, or to send a field representative to assist you in developing the outlet.

Often, a franchise agreement is struck before there is even a site for the proposed outlet. If that's the case, be sure the deadline for opening the business gives you enough time to evaluate potential sites, negotiate a lease, and secure financing. In addition, you'll have to obtain business licenses, signs, and inventory. Negotiate for more time, if you think you really need it. Providing your request is reasonable, the franchisor should be moderately flexible on this issue.

For example, let's say you are considering a franchise to open a car rental agency, and the franchise agreement calls for you to open for business within sixty days. You will need a business loan to finance the outlet. You know a bank that will lend you the money, but it will take ninety days to process the loan application. Considering all the other things you must accomplish before opening—obtaining a site, ordering vehicles, hiring employees, etc.—you ask your franchisor to extend the deadline to 120 days. If you are serious about buying the franchise, the franchisor will probably amend the agreement to give you the time you need. But if you ask for nine months or a year, most likely the negotiations will fall apart.

From the franchisor's point of view, the deadline for developing the outlet encourages rapid market penetration in a new area. He doesn't want the territory sitting idle once he has awarded a franchise. But as a prospective franchisee, you want the deadline to be realistic in the light of business conditions in your locality.

Besides placing a deadline on opening the outlet, the franchise agreement should state exactly who selects the site. Will the franchisor determine the best location for your business? Or will he merely offer advice? Will you be responsible for picking the site? Or will a third party, such as a property developer or realtor, decide where the business will be located?

As a franchisee, you want the benefit of the franchisor's experience in the business. He knows the right customer demographics, traffic flow, and environment for the outlet. On the other hand, you might have a better grasp of the local economic conditions.

Some franchisors who say they will select a site actually contract with a commercial realtor or property manager to recommend an appropriate site. Indeed, a realtor has ready access to suitable properties. But does he have your best interests at heart? Will he focus on sites offering the highest commission or on some other self-serving benefit?

These issues may seem minor at the time, but they can easily become major problems after the franchise agreement is signed. For example, let's say you select your own site for the outlet. A few months later, the business falls into adverse financial straits. You blame your franchisor for failing to provide ongoing assistance, as promised. But, to your aggravation, the franchisor argues that your business is failing only because you selected the wrong site.

Now consider the opposite side of that coin. Let's assume you're the franchisor. As part of your program, you select the site for your franchisee's outlet. Despite your best efforts, one of your franchises fails, plagued by mismanagement and neglect. But in court, the franchisee's attorneys claim the problem was that you picked a bad location.

The solution is to make sure there's a meeting of minds before any site is selected. Both franchisor and franchisee should approve the site in writing before a lease is signed.

8. *Image and Conduct*

This section of the agreement spells out your obligations to maintain the franchisor's presumably high standards of image and conduct. For example, you might be obligated to keep the outlet clean and orderly, comply with certain merchandising standards, maintain adequate insurance coverage, and obey all laws and ordinances which apply to the business.

On the surface, these guidelines seem innocuous enough. After all, uniformity *is* the primary component in franchise success, and without the ability to enforce uniform standards, the competitive advantage of a franchise dissipates in its entirety. Ironically, these very contract provisions relating to quality, cleanliness, and appearance are the classic parents of franchise dispute, disorder, and distress.

Why? Because a franchisor's attorney sometimes devises these conditions as a "safety valve" for ridding the organization of a rogue franchisee. The list of standards may be so inclusive that practically any outlet could be found in violation at any given time.

A crooked poster, a wrinkled menu, a smudged uniform, or an unemptied ashtray could technically put you in default of the franchise agreement. In the past, some franchisors have used tiny spots on window panes, gum wrappers on restroom floors, and salt granules on tabletops as excuses for forcefully terminating a franchise.

Over the last several decades, hundreds of franchise disputes have centered on this volatile issue, prompting several states to pass legislation granting additional rights to franchisees. Today, a franchisor must allow a franchisee a reasonable opportunity to correct the default. In some states, the law prohibits *any* involuntary termination of a franchise for a default in the franchisor's standards of image and cleanliness.

Besides mandatory standards, the agreement may also spell out how much insurance you must carry. Be certain your insurance carrier or agent understands your obligations and can comply exactly. Many carriers simply do not insure franchises at all. The agreement usually requires the franchisor to be named as an additional insured party on your business liability policy.

9. *Advertising and Marketing*

Most franchise agreements will require you to use only advertising materials and media which were developed or approved by the franchisor. As a result, you will probably be limited as to the type of advertising programs you may conduct. For instance, the agreement may give the franchisor the right to prohibit you from using such items as pens, paper weights, or calendars with photographs of naked ladies to promote your franchise.

You might find this restriction vaguely cloaked in such generalized language as "materials which the franchisor, in its sole discretion, may deem unsuitable." Ask the franchisor exactly what kinds of advertising materials he considers "unsuitable." Besides the ones he *doesn't* want you to use, what advertising media *are* approved for promoting your business? Are those media readily available in your locality? Are they as effective in your market as in others? Are they as affordable?

For example, let's say you are considering a franchise to operate a financial counseling business. Based on his past success, the franchisor requires you to spend most of your advertising budget on radio and television ads. But what if those media are two or three times more costly in your market than in most others? Does the franchisor have an alternative advertising plan?

10. *Reports and Audits*

The typical franchise agreement requires you to maintain all the books and records required to document your tax liability and determine your royalty payments. In addition, you may have to prepare periodic financial statements and submit copies to your franchisor.

The agreement may also give the franchisor the right to audit your records at any time. From his point of view, it's important to be able to verify the accuracy of royalty payments. The right to conduct an audit is an integral and necessary safeguard against cheating.

As a prospective franchisee, you should ask: Who pays for the audit? It's one thing to demand an accounting, another to make you bear the cost. An audit by a public accounting firm is expensive. A good compromise is for the franchisor to pay the cost unless the audit uncovers a significant discrepancy or problem. The amount of the discrepancy should be stated in the franchise agreement. Here's an example:

If as a result of the audit a discrepancy in excess of three and one half percent (3.5%) is found to exist, then Franchisee shall pay all costs incurred in connection with the audit.

This kind of arrangement protects both parties. It protects the franchisor against the possibility of cheating by franchisees, and it protects you against frivolous and costly audits.

11. *Assignment of the Franchise*

Most franchise agreements will restrict your ability to sell your franchise to someone else. If for some reason you decide to sell the business, the buyer may have to meet with the franchisor's approval. The term most often used in a franchise agreement is "assignment" of the franchise. Assignment means any change in ownership, whether by sale or transfer. When you sell, or otherwise transfer ownership of the business, the new owner is thus the "assignee."

Who are the potential assignees of your franchise? Besides someone who buys the business, your heirs or beneficiaries might also become assignees, in the event of your death or disability. So, when a franchisor says your franchise may not be assigned without his approval, the right of your heirs to inherit the business may be at stake.

The franchisor may also reserve the "right of first refusal" to buy your franchise. This means that if you decide to sell the business, or if you should pass away while you own it, the franchisor is first in line to purchase the franchise. But he also has the right to refuse, clearing the way for a sale to someone else.

If your franchisor has the right of first refusal, you must offer it for sale to him before anyone else. He will have the right to buy the business for the same price and on the same conditions as any other buyer. For example, let's say you already own a franchise, and someone offers you $300,000 for your business. Before you can accept the offer, you must give the franchisor an opportunity to buy the franchise at the same price. If the franchisor accepts, you have no choice but to sell the business to him for $300,000. If he declines, you may proceed with the sale to the original buyer—assuming, of course, he meets with franchisor's approval.

It's not difficult to understand why a franchisor wants to have control over the sale of one of its franchises. Primarily, he wants to protect the franchise from falling into the hands of an unqualified party. After all, his company invests a great deal of time, effort, and money to recruit, train, and establish a suitable franchisee. He can hardly afford to have the business end up in the possession of someone who does not meet the standard qualifications of other franchisees.

Be sure you understand your franchisor's rights regarding assignment of the franchise. Those rights invariably restrict yours. For example, if you become disabled, the agreement may require you to sell or transfer the business to someone else. If you fail to assign the franchise within a designated period, your franchisor may have the right to take it from you without your permission.

The provisions for assignment also affect franchises operated as a corporation. A franchisor grants franchises to individuals, based on their personal traits, not to business entities such as corporations. When you incorporate, technically you are assigning the franchise to another party.

The agreement may place certain restrictions on your ability to assign your franchise to a corporation:

> As the franchisee, you must remain in control of the business, i.e., as the majority stockholder and chief executive of the corporation.
>
> You must disclose the names of all directors, stockholders, and officers to the franchisor.
>
> The franchisor may have the right to approve any sale or transfer of the stock.

12. *Renewal*

Most, but not all, franchises have a definite term. In other words, they expire after a certain period of time, and must be renewed. Five percent of the franchise agreements currently in force do not have a definite term, meaning that the franchisee's rights never expire. About half of all franchise agreements in use today have a term of ten years.

The agreement usually gives you the right to renew the franchise for another term as the end of the first term approaches. However, to renew the franchise you must usually sign a new agreement. That agreement may not be the same as the one you originally signed. In this way, franchisors can periodically "update" their franchise programs, by changing the terms and conditions of the franchise agreements as they come up for renewal.

The shorter the term, the more flexibility the franchisor has to make changes in its organization. On the other hand, as a prospective franchisee making a substantial investment in the franchise, you deserve the opportunity to reap just rewards. It may take a business as long as three years to begin turning a profit. If the franchise term is only five years, you hardly have enough time to realize a decent return.

13. *Termination*

This section of the agreement spells out the rights of both parties to terminate the contract. For example, if you abandon the business, or are convicted of a felony, the franchisor may have the right to take the franchise from you. On the other hand, you may have the right to terminate the contract if the franchisor fails to fulfill his obligations.

Many franchise agreements say that a franchisor can terminate the franchise unilaterally if you declare bankruptcy. However, you should be aware that, under the Federal Bankruptcy Law, bankruptcy alone may not be used as an excuse to repossess your franchise. But if you fail to keep the doors open for business, you risk losing your investment for "abandoning the franchise."

State laws vary regarding the franchisor's right to terminate a franchise agreement. *No matter what your franchise agreement says, the local statute or ordinance is binding on your franchisor.* For example, the California Franchise Investment Protection Law forbids franchisors from terminating an agreement without "good cause." Good cause is defined as a failure to provide due notice regarding a dispute or default, or a failure to allow the franchisee ample opportunity to correct such a dispute or default. If you live in Mississippi, and a franchisor terminates the agreement, he must be prepared to repurchase your inventory of goods.

For example, let's say you buy a franchise to sell a product which is exclusively distributed by your franchisor. You order a large opening inventory of products. When the shipment arrives, your franchisor can't suddenly cancel the agreement and stick you with a warehouse full of goods. This law helps to assure that franchisors are genuinely interested in your personal success, not merely in taking advantage of you as a captive customer.

14. *Obligations Upon Termination or Expiration*

If, for any reason, you and your franchisor should part ways, this section of the agreement spells out your obligations. For example, you may be required to return the franchise manual and cease using any of the franchisor's trademarks. You might also have to give up your business phone number.

Most agreements contain a "covenant not to compete." In the covenant, you pledge not to compete with the franchisor in the same business after the agreement expires or is terminated. You should be aware that such covenants are not valid in some states, including California, the largest franchise market.

15. *Enforcement and Construction*

Every good agreement has a morass of perplexing legal terminology dealing with issues like" severability," "substitution," "governing law," and "binding effect. "

The "severability" clause assures that the contract remains in force though part of the agreement may happen to be struck down in court. For example, let's say you sign a franchise agreement which contains a covenant not to compete. Later, a court rules that all such covenants are unenforceable in your state. Even though this part of your franchise agreement may be unenforceable, the rest of the agreement remains in full force and effect.

A "substitution" clause simply means that if the local law is different from any provision in the agreement, that law is automatically substituted for the offending provision. Assume, for instance, that you sign a franchise agreement which states that to renew the contract, you must notify the franchisor at least one year before the expiration date.

However, the law in your state allows you to wait sixty days before the contract expires to make up your mind. In this case, the sixty-day requirement mandated by law is automatically substituted for the one-year requirement in the agreement.

The "governing law" clause stipulates which state's laws will be used to interpret the agreement in the event of a dispute. Almost invariably, this is the state in which the franchisor is headquartered.

The basic parts of a franchise agreement are illustrated in the sample franchise agreement in the Appendix. As you evaluate an agreement, you should seek the assistance of an attorney with ample franchise experience. If your own attorney doesn't have the appropriate background, ask him or her to recommend a lawyer or firm that has more experience handling franchise cases.

It is worth repeating that the franchisor's lawyers have drafted the contract to provide maximum advantage for the franchisor, often cloaked in innocent-sounding verbiage. An agreement between a franchisor and franchisee falls under special rules and interpretations that are different from other types of contracts.

14
GETTING STARTED IN A FRANCHISE BUSINESS

"Ideas are easy. Implementation is hard."
                                    Guy Kawasaki

Despite the rigors of researching, investigating, evaluating, applying for, negotiating, and financing a franchise, signing a franchise agreement is just the beginning of the adventure. The next challenge will be to organize the business, select a location, complete the franchisor's training program, study the operating manual, develop the site, and prepare the outlet for opening. Although your franchisor may help you with some or all of the details, it will help you to have a clear picture of the myriad responsibilities that lie ahead. And in some cases, your franchisor may not tell you everything you need to know.

Many would-be entrepreneurs view a franchise only as an investment opportunity, without realizing the amount of hard work it takes to develop a business and make it successful. On the opposite side of that coin, some franchisors are better at motivating franchisees to invest than teaching them the ropes. This chapter will help you come to grips with the realities of starting and managing a business, and organize your time and energies effectively during the crucial start-up period.

Organizing the Business

One of the first decisions faced by a business owner is

the form of organization under which to conduct the business. There are legal as well as tax considerations that must enter into this decision. A wise franchisee seeks and relies on competent counsel, such as a small business attorney, CPA, or other licensed advisor, before deciding on a particular form of organization.

Normally, a business may be conducted as one of three entities: a sole proprietorship, a partnership, or a corporation.

Tax Considerations

A business operated as a sole proprietorship does not pay income taxes. Instead, the sole proprietor reports profits or losses from the business on his own income tax return.

Profits from a corporation are usually taxed both to the corporation and again to the individual shareholders when profits are distributed as dividends. A competent attorney should be consulted to determine the legal, organizational, and tax implications of incorporation. Most franchise agreements stipulate certain conditions and actions required when a franchise business is organized as a corporation.

Following is a general discussion of the distinguishing traits, advantages, and drawbacks to each form of business organization.

A Franchise Operated as a Sole Proprietorship

The sole proprietorship is the simplest form of business organization. The business has no separate identity from its owner's. Its liabilities are the owner's personal liabilities. Income from a sole proprietorship is part of the owner's total gross reportable income.

The proprietor must report all income from the business on federal and state tax returns. In addition, the owner is subject to self-employment tax.

The Internal Revenue Service allows sole proprietors to deduct such expenses as advertising, bank charges, equipment depreciation, insurance, office supplies, rent, utilities, and other costs of doing business.

A Franchise Operated as a Partnership

In a general partnership, each partner shares both the liabilities and the assets of the business. Each is taxed according to his or her share of the profits. As with a sole proprietor, the partner must report all income form the business on state and federal tax returns, and may have to pay self-employment tax in addition to income tax.

The partnership must also submit a separate tax return disclosing the profits, draws, and advances paid out to the partners. Similarly, partners are jointly and severably liable for all liabilities of the business.

In a limited liability partnership, only the general partners have direct responsibility for the debts and liabilities of the business. The limited partners receive a share of the profits, which are then taxed as ordinary income.

A Franchise Operated as a Corporation

When a business is operated as a corporation, profits are taxed to the corporation. When profits are distributed in the form of dividends, these are taxed to the individual shareholders. However, the corporation itself is a separate entity—another "person" in the view of the law. In general, the corporation, not its shareholders, is responsible for the liabilities of the business. In some instances, the officers and directors of a small corporation may be held liable for debts of the business and the actions of employees.

In a sub-Chapter S corporation, the corporation is not taxed, but shareholders must report their share of profits and losses on their gross income statements when reporting tax liabilities.

To form a corporation, all shareholders must transfer money, property, or both, to the corporation in exchange for stock entitling each shareholder to a portion of the profit. As a general rule, stock should not be exchanged for services. But corporate shares may be issued in return for cancellation of indebtedness for past services.

A competent attorney experienced in small businesses and closely held corporations should be consulted in all matters pertaining to the formation of a corporation, issuance of stock, and reporting of tax liabilities.

Usually, a franchisee's election to incorporate is governed by certain provisions in the franchise agreement. A franchise is normally granted to an individual, in reliance on his or her character, aptitude, business skill, management ability, and other qualities. The franchisee must assign the franchise to the newly formed corporation. The assignment usually requires the franchisor's prior approval, but approval will not be reasonably withheld.

The following stipulations are typical in most franchise agreements:

1. Control of ownership

The franchisee you must own and control the majority of the ownership (equity) and voting power of the corporation. This provision protects both the franchisor and the franchisee against the involuntary wrenching of control from by other shareholders.

2. Management control

The franchisee must actively manage and direct the corporation. In other words, the franchisee must be the corporation's chief executive officer.

3. Exclusive business

The corporation must not be engaged in any other business besides the franchise business.

4. Stock legends

The stock certificates of the corporation may not bear any trademark or symbol of the franchisor, unless they are accompanied by a statement that the stock is stock in a franchise (not stock in the franchising corporation).

All stock certificates must bear a legend stating that the transfer of the stock is limited, or such other legend as is required by the appropriate state or federal corporate regulatory agency for stock in a corporate franchisee.

5. Personal guarantee

The franchisee usually sign a personal guarantee stating that he or she will be empowered to act on behalf of the new corporation and will personally guarantee all the liabilities, debts, and obligations under the franchise agreement.

6. Corporate documents

Upon organizing the corporation, the franchisee must usually submit the following items to the franchisor:

- A resolution of the Board of Directors stating full acknowledgement and approval of the franchise agreement

- A list of all shareholders, stating their names, addresses, and the number of shares owned by each

- A list of all officers and directors
- A copy of the articles of incorporation, corporate bylaws, and any other pertinent resolutions.

Selecting the Site for Your Business

After organizing the business, the selection of a site for the outlet is usually the next decision faced by a business-format franchisee. A principal business address must be secured before certain licenses or permits required to conduct the business may be obtained. Moreover, location may have a bearing on the outlet's success or failure.

Some franchisors select the locations for their franchisees' outlets or, as an alternative, offer to perform this service for a fee. Others, though they may not actively assist with securing a site, may reserve the right to approve the franchisee's selection. In such cases, you may be required to submit three to five potential sites for the franchisor's review and approval.

The following considerations influence the selection of a site for a typical retail or commercial franchise outlet:

Zoning

As with other businesses, the outlet must comply with local zoning laws, statutes, and ordinances. Among other considerations, zoning may affect fire inspections, health inspections, business permits, and other licenses or permits relating to the site.

Security

Your business files and records are confidential. All information, correspondence, records, and customer lists dealing with the franchise business should be adequately safeguarded against potential abuse, including theft. Security from loss by fire, flood, etc. should also be a consideration, because insurance alone will not provide adequate compensation if your business records and files are destroyed.

Space requirements

The franchisor may require the outlet to be situated in a particular type of facility, such as a shopping mall, business park, high rise complex, strip center, or standalone retail site. As a new franchisee, you must anticipate both interior and exterior space requirements. If a long-term lease is required, future expansion needs should also be taken into consideration.

Allow for ample parking for both customers and employees. Employee parking should be situated away from the entrance to the place of business, providing maximum parking convenience for customers.

Fixtures and improvements

As you evaluate prospective sites, seek the answers to the following questions:

What are the existing provisions for lighting, heating, ventilating, air conditioning, and parking?

What share of these costs will the franchisee be required to undertake?

Your outlet's exterior sign is one of a franchisee's principal advertising media. Where applicable, the site should allow the outlet sign to be prominently displayed and easily visible to passing traffic in both directions. If you will operate a retail outlet, avoid sites that are located away from the main thoroughfare, e.g., in the back of a business park where the exterior sign is hidden from passing traffic.

Environment and Image

It is important in most franchise businesses, to select an attractive building surrounded by other businesses which project a favorable image on the outlet as well as the franchise. Even though a franchisor may not require the outlet to be situated in the most expensive and prestigious building complex in a given locality, the franchisee is responsible for maintaining the high standard of image and quality of the franchise organization.

The site should be professional in appearance, clean, attractive, and preferably, located in a well-maintained area. On a personal note, franchisees should also consider that they will be spending the majority of their waking hours in their franchise outlet. Will the location provide a comfortable environment for the business's employees? Will customers also feel comfortable?

Surrounding area

The overall image of the surroundings, the proximity to major customer groups, accessibility of major traffic arteries, and visibility, all also may influence the outlet's success. The franchisee's own personal image is derived, in part, from the company he or she keeps. Similarly, the business's image will be derived, in part, from the surrounding businesses. An office in a modern shopping mall or business park projects a professional, success-oriented image. Conversely, a business located in a run-down strip center or warehouse area presents a poor image.

Proximity to customers

In most businesses, to some extent location will determine the makeup of the outlet's primary customers. For example, a business located near upper-income residential areas is more likely to attract consumers who have ample disposable income. A business located in an industrial park or high rise complex caters to business customers. A franchisee who selects a strip center or shopping mall for the outlet will be perceived as catering to housewives and shoppers.

Access to thoroughfares

One important attribute of the outlet site is accessibility to major thoroughfares. Convenience is a key factor in the consumer's decision to patronize retail establishments. Access to major arteries and thoroughfares is a substantial advantage, particularly in a large metropolitan area.

Most franchisors have a profile of the ideal outlet site, with specifications for space requirements, lease provisions, visibility and access from major thoroughfares, and other considerations. As mentioned previously, many franchisors rely on local realtors or property managers to select sites in geographical markets where the franchisors may have limited prior experience.

Because site selection is often a major factor in the success or failure of a business, the matter of who chooses the location—and how—sometimes becomes an issue in franchisor-franchisee disputes. If a franchise outlet fails, one of the first argument the franchisee's attorney is likely to raise is that the franchisor selected or approved a poor location. Yet, the franchisor's know-how and experience are integral components of the franchise relationship, and, reasonably, no franchisee should be expected to assume the responsibility of site selection without some form of guidance or assistance.

The Franchise Operating Manual

The franchisor's know-how and operating standards are usually documented in a series of publications collectively referred to as the franchise operating manual. The Franchise Disclosure Documents refers to operating manuals in the instructions for completing Section XI-C of the disclosure document:

> *(3) Describe any operating manual provided to the franchisee to assist the franchisee and his employees in the operation of the franchised business and whether the franchisor retains the right to change the terms of the manual and, if so, under what circumstances.*

By providing an operating manual, a franchisor fulfills an important condition of the federal definition of a franchise relationship. You will recall that, under the FTC rules, a franchise is any commercial relationship involving a licensed trademark, payment of a fee, and "significant control or assistance."

Normally, an operating manual is regarded as a trade secret of the franchisor. Consequently, most franchise agreements obligate the franchisee to keep the contents confidential. A typical operating manual is loaned, not given, to the franchisee for the term of the franchise agreement. Upon expiration of the franchise, all copies of the manual in the franchisee's possession must be returned to the franchisor. The franchise agreement may obligate the managers and employees of the franchisee's outlet to sign confidentiality oaths, preventing disclosure of any portion of the operating manual to unauthorized parties.

A typical franchise agreement gives the franchisor the right to modify the manual periodically, providing that the modifications do not alter any of the franchisee's rights.

Franchisees are usually bound to adhere to any mandatory policies, procedures, specifications, and standards published in the operating manual.

Although there is no standard franchise operating manual, a good manual touches on virtually aspect of starting, developing, staffing, managing, operating, and promoting the franchise business. The publication may be divided into a series of volumes, each devoted to a separate topic, such as marketing or daily operating procedures. It is common for managers and rank-and-file employees to have separate manuals, as well.

Many franchisors provide complete start-up assistance or a fully developed "turn-key" business. However, in many cases, franchisors rely on their franchisees to exercise independence and initiative to establish the business and prepare the outlet for opening. If that is the case, the following checklist will help you cover all the bases and, if necessary, fill in the gaps between what you need to know and what you'll learn at franchise training school.

Business Organization

_ Corporate documents
_ Partnership documents
_ Business license
_ Trademark registration/trade name permit
_ Federal employer's ID number
_ Payroll tax forms
_ Payroll tax deposit account
_ Business checking account
_ Business license
_ Zoning use permit
_ Fire inspection
_ Health inspection
_ Safety inspection
_ Credit card services

_ Check verification services
_ Business liability insurance
_ Fire and damage insurance
_ Motor vehicle insurance
_ Business liability insurance
_ Employee group insurance
_ Life insurance
_ Construction permit(s)
_ Sign permit(s)

Site Development

_ Utility deposits
_ Telephone deposits
_ Telephone installation
_ Inventory Fixtures
_ Storage Fixtures
_ Wall decorations
_ Locks
_ Security/alarm system
_ Exterior signs
_ Equipment and furnishings
_ Vehicle lease(s)

Finance

_ Business Plan
_ Loan application
_ Vendor contacts
_ Bank accounts
_ Computer hardware system
_ Software installation and training
_ Invoice file
_ Expense file
_ Asset file
_ Liability file

_ Travel & entertainment expense file
_ Employee file
_ Social security file
_ Payroll tax depository
_ Tax files
_ Banking procedures
_ Business checks
_ Business forms
_ Petty cash fund
_ Rate sheet
_ Credit file
_ Office supplies

Public Relations and Promotion

_ Competition analysis
_ Media Contact list
_ Business forms
_ Yellow pages advertising
_ Hand-outs and fliers
_ Newspaper/magazine ads
_ Television commercials
_ Radio commercials
_ Stationery
_ Business cards
_ Grand Opening plan
_ Grand Opening invitations
_ Press release stationery
_ Grand Opening press release
_ Personnel Policy Manual
_ Mailing labels
_ Advertising Budget
_ Advertising calendar
_ Advertising plan
_ Reception planning

_ Reception invitations
_ Grand Opening

15
WHY FRANCHISES FAIL

"The only real mistake is the one from which we learn nothing."
Henry Ford

Many of the precautions and disputes discussed throughout this book highlight some of the most prominent reasons why a franchise might fail. Depending on one's perspective, the causes may be regarded as franchisor-related, franchisee-related, or extrinsic.

Franchisor-related

Largely because of investment hype and the persuasive rhetoric of franchisors and their representatives, when a franchise business fails, the franchisee is apt to find fault with the franchisor.

Inadequate Support

There are a number of reasons why a franchisor's support mechanism is not always sufficient to prevent an outlet from closing. When a franchise chain expands too rapidly, without investing in an adequate support structure, the result is inevitably a tide of outlet failures. Some franchisors, to be sure, simply have unqualified support representatives, or ineffective systems in place. Franchisees typically have little or no prior experience in the franchisor's industry and, as such, require not only the franchisor's trademark, know how, and system, but also personal and professional guidance in the day-to-day operation of the business.

Poor Location

Many businesses, especially retail and food service outlets, fail because of their location. The elements of visibility, access, and neighborhood are essential to the survival of these types of enterprises. Many outlets located in shopping malls that once experienced high volume have gone out of business as a result of the failure of the mall itself.

Inadequate Territory

When a franchisee's restricted territory has insufficient numbers of potential customers, the outlet is doomed before it opens. This problem also arises when a franchisor establishes too many franchises in close proximity to one another. As franchise chains merge or are acquired by other companies engaged in franchising, *de facto* competition often emerges to the detriment of existing franchisees.

Inadequate Marketing

Undoubtedly, some franchisees expect customers to begin walking through the entrance as soon as the outlet opens. They do so in reliance on the franchisor's ability to recruit customers. Unfortunately, there is disagreement among the franchise community about exactly who is responsible for recruiting customers: the franchisee or the franchisor. Ultimately, one or the other—or both—need to be able to compete successfully for the hearts, minds, and disposable income of the consumers of their products and services.

Market Saturation

Fundamentally, every business competes not only against other businesses in its industry or market, but against all other possible uses of the customer's money. The problem is compounded when the number of similar businesses is so great that even if all were to share equally in customer spending, none of them could generate enough sales to survive.

Insolvency

One of the hazards faced by franchising companies that over-extend their resources by expanding too rapidly is, simply stated, running out of money. The truth is that some franchisors are actually under-capitalized, relying primarily on a continuing flow of initial fees to sustain their operations. Franchise operations whose shares are traded on the stock market are especially vulnerable to unexpected downturns resulting from market fluctuations and current events.

Franchisee-related

Not surprisingly, outlet failures are likely to be viewed through a franchisor's eyes as the responsibility of the franchisee.

Lack of Suitability

Some franchisees, no matter how passionate they may be about the product, brand, or industry, are basically not suited to the business. Some may lack the flexibility needed to evolve with the business over time, while others are simply incapable of managing or retaining staff.

Insufficient Planning

The cliche that "a failure to plan is a plan to fail" is nonetheless true. Despite a franchisor's brand and system, franchise outlets routinely fail because of poor planning by franchisees.

Insufficient Capital

Perhaps the most commonly overlooked aspect of a franchise investment is the working capital required to sustain the franchisee and the business until the outlet begins to be profitable. Undercapitalization is a prescription for failure in any business. Even though the initial investment is itemized in the Franchise Disclosure document, franchisees often underestimate actual operating costs.

Weathering unexpected situations without a financial cushion can be problematic even for an established franchise.

Bad Management

Many franchisees who aren't by nature good managers themselves fail to hire a good manager to run the business. Employee disputes resulting from bad management are a major cause of outlet failure. In extreme cases, outlets have been forced to close because of dishonest managers or employees extracting money from the business illegally.

Complacency

If the franchisee fails to evolve with the market, the business ultimately becomes irrelevant. Franchises have failed because the owner became more interested in a side business or a preoccupation such as gambling or travel.

Failure to Follow the System

Some franchisees come to believe that they are more capable of running the business than the franchisor. When the franchisee's management style and ideals are at odds with the franchisor's brand and system, the outcome is generally an unhappy one for both franchisor and franchisee.

Extrinsic Causes

Franchises are equally vulnerable to perils posed by extrinsic phenomena such as shifts in population, consumer buying habits, and unexpected economic downturns.

Population Shift

To some degree, virtually every retail business is affected by population trends. The post-World War II baby boom created what became the largest, most affluent consumer group in history. As this huge spending machine advanced in age, entire industries rose and fell. Another, smaller baby boom occurred in the 1970s, when the U.S. population increased by 3.15 million babies every year.

Within the next 25 years, sales of products currently purchased by super-consumers will decline dramatically, affecting such industries as real estate, travel, hospitality, automobiles, and services targeting the aging. The popular term for this event horizon is the "demographic cliff." The resulting surplus of goods and services will result in widespread outlet closures and unemployment in numerous industries that currently rely on this population group.

E-commerce

The rise of product sales via the internet has already impacted retail businesses in the electronics, apparel, book, and small appliance industries. As of this writing, 61% of all retail sales transactions involve the web. The list of the world's largest companies, formerly topped by automobile manufacturers, oil producers, or electronics companies, is now led by online retailers.

Franchisors in virtually every market category face an imposing challenge to adapt rapidly and adeptly to the consumer's continually increasing preference for internet-enabled purchasing.

The Sharing Economy

The rise of such gray-market industries as online marketplaces, ride-sharing services, and short-term room rentals has dramatically impacted traditional retail and service sales. In 2018, Amazon surged to become the largest retailer, Uber the largest ground transportation service, and AirBnB the leading lodging organization.

Social media websites serve as a stage for consumer reaction and reviews. Comments on Facebook, Twitter, Pinterest, or Linkedin have the power to boost or sabotage sales. News reports of negative incidents have caused the sales of entire franchise chains to plummet, resulting in losses in the millions.

Cultural Influences

Changing consumer buying habits resulting from shifts in fashions and trends pose a peril for most retail operations. When fast food sales burgeoned in the 1960s and 1970s, it was predictable that weight loss and physical fitness would become popular in the 1980s. Completing the cycle, as fast food once again became fashionable, fitness businesses struggled to remain solvent.

Economic Influences

Unexpected upswings and downturns can occur in any industry. Few experts expected the computer industry to plummet in the mid 1980s or predicted the crisis in the real estate and banking industries in 2008. The economic downturn from 2009 to 2015 created a tsunami of outlet closures in franchising. Major chains once thought too big to fail collapsed almost overnight. Others weathered the storm by adapting their product offerings and prices to changing economic conditions, reducing outlets and staff, and reorganizing their companies.

16
FRANCHISING AND THE FUTURE

"Tomorrow belongs to the people who prepare for it today."
                                            African proverb

In franchising, the future is as important as the past. The average term of a franchise agreement is ten years, during which time market conditions, economic variables, and consumer buying behavior are likely to change dramatically.

Financial experts use simple logic to track trends. To illustrate, consider the logic used by a commodities trader to gauge the effect of interest rates on lumber futures. When interest rates drop, real estate sales tend to increase, creating demand in the housing market. As the supply of available homes shrinks, new home construction begins to climb. Lumber mills are generally idle except during periods of peak demand, so the existing supply of seasoned lumber is quickly exhausted. The resulting shortage drives lumber prices up.

Conversely, when interest rates rise, real estate sales drop, a housing surplus develops, new home construction declines, and lumber mills, which were active while construction was soaring, produce a new surplus, driving the price of lumber down.

To some extent, this type of reasoning can be applied to franchise investments. For example, following periods of low population growth, the market for children's and infants' products may be expected to decline. On the other hand, when a baby boom is in progress, the economic outlook is favorable for day care centers and children's apparel stores.

By paying attention to consumer habits and economic developments, it is possible to track some trends over a relatively long period of time. However, no matter how logical or scientific it may be, any prediction about industry trends is basically informed guesswork.

Still, a franchise decision should be based not merely on a franchisor's track record but also on some sense of the future. With that objective in mind, it is worthwhile to examine some past, present, and future trends that may influence franchising and impact franchise businesses.

An Aging Population

The "super-consumers" born between 1945 and 1960 have now reached the peak age of their personal purchasing power. As of this writing, they are the main buyers of cars, homes, and airline tickets, and control eighty percent of all the money in savings accounts.

A crystal ball isn't needed to foresee that, as this affluent generation continues to enter retirement, a huge demand will unfold for products and services that cater to older adults. However, it is inevitable that, when this generation dwindles in importance, the economic landscape will undergo a major, potentially devastating, transformation.

An obvious example is the travel and hospitality industry. Every minute of every day, somewhere in North America, someone boards an airplane, checks into a hotel, rents a car, plans a cruise trip, purchases a train ticket, or makes some other type of travel arrangement. According to a study conducted by the World Travel and Tourism Council, the travel industry is currently the largest individual industry in the world and the largest contributor to global economic development.

Worldwide, the travel industry generates more than $2.5 trillion in gross annual revenues, representing 5.5 percent of the world economy. This industry also provides jobs for more than 112 million people, or one of every fifteen employees in the world. Statistics show that the average American household spends more money on travel than on any other item except groceries.

Two factors will fuel the travel and hospitality industries over the next two decades—the expansion of the global economy and the graying of the American population. Business travelers now account for two-thirds of all travel industry revenues. From 1982 through 1992, international travel tripled. Business relations between companies in different countries will increase significantly as economic unions are developed and trade pacts are implemented.

As the most affluent consumer group continues to age, the popularity of vacation travel will also increase. Consumers who are reaching retirement age now have more leisure time and money to spend than the retiring population groups of the past. This phenomenon augers well for such industries as the hospitality and car rental industries.

The hospitality industry is made up of businesses that provide lodging, food and beverages, and related services to travelers. Hotels, motels, and resorts make up the world's seventh largest industry, generating over $36 billion in annual sales. Automotive rental outlets are among the oldest franchise businesses and provide franchisees with the benefits of national advertising, centralized reservations, and strong name recognition.

In general, the next ten years will see a trend away from such purchases as homes and automobiles, to increased spending on household equipment and furniture. The market for food and beverages will continue to shift from families to working people and elderly consumers.

Studies indicate that Baby Boomers tend to be more health-conscious, active, and fitness-oriented than previous generations. The vast majority want to remain independent and live in their own homes rather than in nursing facilities.

The majority intends to continue working beyond their retirement years.

These traits support the notion of a surge in demand for aging-related products and services. It is foreseeable that new chains will emerge devoted to adult day care centers, senior fitness clubs, anti-aging centers, elderly employment services, geriatric counseling and care, and companion services for the elderly.

The demand for in-home food products and services will grow as an alternative to going out—based on both convenience and value. Targeting consumers aged 60 and over will be crucial to the profitability of food service chains. These consumers seek products that provide convenience and indulgence at justified prices. Studies of consumer buying behavior indicate that indulgence is important to senior consumers: for example, being waited on in a store or having products delivered to the home.

However, the window of opportunity is clearly limited. As the aging super-consumer generation passes, the demand for related products and services could plummet. There will be far more hotel rooms than guests and more rental cars than travelers. The consumer generation that will follow is smaller in number and, statistically, less prone to traveling away from home.

Real estate will also be impacted by the passing of the super-consumer generation. There will be more homes and apartments than people to occupy them, either through purchase or rental. Currently, new home construction and sales of existing properties are in a state of flux in response to interest rates, available inventory, and the creditworthiness of buyers. Over 90% of all real estate transactions involve a mortgage or other type of loan. As illustrated by the collapse of the real estate and banking industries in 2008, the industries are closely tied.

One has only to look at the past and present to discern the influence of the approaching "demographic cliff." When today's super-consumers were infants, mobile diaper services and toy store franchises became leading players. In the following decades, outlets devoted to apparel, sporting goods, and entertainment began to prosper. A multi-billion dollar music industry arose based on the cultural tastes of teenaged and adolescent consumers.

As the Baby Boomers entered the workforce, their consumption habits began to shift to adult-oriented apparel, automobiles, hair styling services, and home improvement products. Eventually, the music stores and trendy fashion boutiques the maturing consumers had once patronized began to fade in popularity.

The Impact of the Sharing Economy

Fundamentally, the sharing economy is a revolt against traditional methods of doing business. The concept has become so widespread and accepted by consumers that its influence in reshaping the economy is inevitable.

The principles are tantalizing to a largely unstudied swath of the public, especially the Gen Z generation:

> Download a phone app.
> Sign up.
> Pay a small fee.
> Start working.
> Benefit from the brand.
> Get customers from the provider.
> Get paid.
> Be your own boss.

The jobs are known as "gigs," styled after the work performed by freelancers in the arts and entertainment fields.

Unlike franchisees, who apply and pay for the same type of privileges, gig sharing operations aren't covered by franchise regulations or, in most cases, even the same regulations that apply to other businesses in the same industry.

Uber, for instance, has influenced a number of municipalities to waive the taxes and fees that legally licensed taxicab companies are obligated to pay. Similarly, AirBnB has influenced local authorities to exclude its participants from the regulations and taxes that pertain to lodging establishments and bed-and-breakfast inns.

As the operations of large corporations are increasingly impacted, there will be intense pressure on governments to enact regulations and controls. To date, the vast fortunes already accumulated by gig sharing providers have enabled them not only to negotiate with local governments, but to manipulate their decisions.

It is not inconceivable that gig sharing could, at some point, completely replace numerous traditional franchise operations, or at least relegate them to second-class citizenship in the hierarchy of startup opportunities.

Already, online auction websites, transportation services, and room-rental operations based on gig sharing have overtaken their traditional franchise rivals in both customer numbers and gross sales.

The Next Consumers

America's youngest generation, "Gen Z"—those born after 1998—are now entering their formative years and rising in influence. At nearly 70 million strong, the eldest members of this consumer group are now entering college or the workforce. As an economic factor, this group will soon become more important than their "Millennial" predecessors.

Millennials, the eldest of which are entering their mid to late 30s, are becoming increasingly employed in middle management roles. In addition to managing other Millennials, they will soon be managing Gen Z employees.

Gen Z is the first generation born literally connected to the internet from the first moment they were able to hold a device. Culturally, they are radically different than Millennials. The future of franchising and the economy beyond the next ten years will lie in the challenge of understanding and adapting to the Gen Z consumer.

To fill the economic gap left by the passing of the super-consumer Baby Boomers, governments will be pressured to increase immigration. By 2030, given the drastic fallout in the number of consumers and workers, it is difficult to imagine that the U.S. economy can be sustained without adding to the working adult population. A new wave of immigrants will be expected to compensate for shortages in the labor force and also pick up the slack in the consumption of goods and services.

This diverse group of consumers will bring new cultural values and traditions on which franchisors of the future will need to focus in order to thrive. The majority will likely make purchasing decisions based on value and culture.

Immigrants are more likely than other Americans to relocate to obtain employment, and also more likely to start their own businesses. Most, however, will take jobs left vacant by the demographic labor shortage. Their disposable income and preferences in food, apparel, and transportation options may well transform the retail culture. Savvy franchisors are already planning for this eventuality, in the realization that the future viability of their businesses depends on the buying behavior of an as-yet unknown and unstudied population.

The Regulatory Future

The adoption and enforcement of regulations have waxed and waned over time, depending on the attitudes of elected officials toward consumer protection. Periods of reduced protection may be viewed as "regulatory winter," and those of increased enforcement as "regulatory spring."

Three major regulatory springs occurred in 1977, 2005, and 2015. When the first round of federal regulations went into effect in June, 1977, more than half of the franchise advertisements in the Wall Street Journal disappeared within a month. Clearly, regulations are important not only to preventing fraud and abuse, but to preserving the integrity of the franchising industry, as well.

Starting in 2016, the federal government began to enter regulatory winter. As a result, the burden of protecting investors shifted to individual states. A predictable consequence is increasing future regulation and enforcement at the state level.

Economic Challenges

It is worth bearing in mind that much of the cheerleading for franchising today is aimed at attracting capital investment, stock sales, funding for start-ups, or sales of products sold by franchise outlets. It is important to keep this fact in mind when evaluating franchise offerings.

The impact of global economic health looms large in any investment decision. Even if a new era of regulation for the financial markets arises, it will not protect global economies from crises.

The price of an object bought, held, or sold for investment or profit experiences a predictable cycle of peaks and valleys. Real estate, securities, and rare metals are typical examples. Increasing demand causes the price to rise. As the object is repeatedly resold for gain, new purchasers join in, creating the illusion that there is no upward limit. At some point, a summit is reached where further price growth can no longer be sustained, due to extreme overvaluation.

This economic principle has been at the root of financial crises throughout human history. As of this writing, investment in the stock market is at an all time high. Predictably, the value of shares continues to be driven by an illusion that there will be no end to stock-market windfalls.

The truth, however, is that interest and investment in stocks will also reach its upward limit, dictated not by regulatory spring but by immutable economic realities. The worst case is a "bubble burst" comparable to the infamous "dot com" and real estate crises that sent global economies into a downward spiral. The best case is a phased adjustment (or in the jargon of stock market analysts a "correction") over a manageable period of time.

The Resilience of Franchises

Throughout the history of franchising, the industry has been exceptionally resilient, though not entirely immune, to economic downturns. When able to adjust to changing market conditions, traditional business-format franchises endure because of consumers' confidence in, and preference for, familiar goods and services. A franchise's proven operational models and built-in support mechanisms increase the owner's chances of weathering tough economic storms.

As a result, independent companies continue to expand into franchising, increasing the number and variety of opportunities. These organizations range from established corporations to company-owned stores and restaurants. Technology will become more conspicuous among franchises as consumer buying behavior continues to shift to the internet.

Of course, it is impossible to predict the future with absolute certainty. Still, the ability to apply the lessons of the past to the attainment of future goals is essential in most endeavors.

As the philosopher Soren Kierkegaard put it,

"Life can only be understood backwards; but it must be lived forwards."

EPILOG

Entrepreneurship is a bold, often exhilarating, adventure involving numerous decisions, both rational and emotional. Anyone considering a franchise investment must recognize from the outset that such a decision is not an exclusively intellectual consideration. There is an emotional investment in any business decision, particularly one that will so profoundly affect someone's life, career, and well-being. Yet, it is important to balance that emotional part against the purely rational aspects of where you are now, where you want to be in the future, and how you are going to get there.

Statistics suggest that a franchise business is more likely to succeed than other independently owned businesses. On the opposite side of that coin, franchisees are twice as likely to be involved in litigation. Although the disclosure document informs prospective franchisees about the proposed investment, it does not completely shield them from potential fraud. The burden of verifying a franchisor's credentials and credibility remains with the prospective franchisee.

Among the factors that influence the sustainability of a franchise organization are the company's financial condition, brand loyalty, number of outlets, ratio of outlet openings to closures, litigation, and, where applicable, stock performance. Other issues, such as customer and employee satisfaction, franchisee relations, use of advanced technology, ability to adapt to market changes, and social media presence, also contribute to the likelihood of success or failure over the long term.

People do not make crucial decisions solely on the basis of information processing and evaluation. They are also influenced by cultural factors, people, and lifestyle. No issue in franchising is more important than the legal, ethical, and financial relationship between franchisors and their franchisees. Most disagreements focus on the mutual rights and obligations of the parties.

In franchising, reading the future is often as important as interpreting the past. No one who considers a franchise investment can afford to ignore the combined influence of social, economic, and cultural trends on the future success of the business. Nevertheless, franchise success is ultimately dependent as much on people as systems and standards. To quote Dee Hock, founder and former CEO of Visa, "An organization, no matter how well designed, is only as good as the people who live and work in it."

Life, it is often said, is the sum of all your choices. Your success or failure in business will hinge on the sum of all your decisions and the people who strive to put them to work, including, first and foremost, yourself.

APPENDIX A

SAMPLE FRANCHISE AGREEMENT

FRANCHISE AGREEMENT

1. Grant of Franchise

A. Widget World Franchise Corporation (the "Franchisor") hereby grants to _____ whose business address is _____ (the "Franchisee") a license to use the trade name "Widget World" and the trade marks associated therewith, and a franchise to operate a Widget World outlet (the "Outlet") in the geographical market identified in Exhibit A of this agreement.

B. Franchisee shall use the trade name and marks in the conduct of a [outlet description], and franchisee's place of business shall incorporate the name Widget World.

C. The name of any corporation operating this franchise may include the name "Widget World" or any other trade mark owned or licensed by franchisor, but only with the written consent of franchisor.

2. Exclusive Territory

Franchisor shall not, while this agreement is in force, conduct a similar operation, or grant a similar franchise to any other franchisee, within the territory defined in Exhibit A.

3. Term

This agreement shall continue for a period of [length of term] years from the date hereof, and shall be automatically renewed for an additional term, unless at least six (6) months before the expiration of this agreement, franchisee gives to franchisor notice in writing of termination at the end of the term.

4. Development and Opening

Within ninety (90) days of the execution of this agreement, franchisee shall do or cause the following to be done:

A. Secure all financing required to develop the outlet;

B. Complete all arrangements for a site for the outlet. Franchisor shall have the right and option to approve the selected site prior to the development and opening of the outlet.

C. Execute a lease for the premises in which the outlet shall be operated, and deliver to the franchisor a true and correct copy;

D. Obtain all licenses and permits required to conduct the business;

E. Obtain all improvements, fixtures, supplies, and inventory.

5. Payments

A. Franchise Fee

Franchisee shall make payment to franchisor the sum of $_____ Dollars ($_____) upon execution of this agreement, receipt of which is hereby acknowledged. In return for this payment, franchisee shall receive the right to do business as a licensed Widget World franchise under the terms of this agreement, and to receive the services and assistance hereinafter set forth. The initial fee shall be fully earned by the franchisor and is nonrefundable.

6. Advertising

A. Franchisee agrees to use all advertising designs, materials, media, and methods preparation described by or which conform to franchisor's standards and specifications.

B. Franchisee shall refrain from using any advertising designs, materials, media, and methods of preparation which do not meet franchisor's standards and specifications.

C. Franchisor shall make available to franchisee any assistance that may be required, based on the experience and judgment of franchisor, in the design, preparation, and placement of advertising and promotional materials for use in local advertising.

D. Franchisor shall administer the Franchisee Cooperative Advertising Fund, and direct the development of all advertising and promotional programs. The content of the advertising, as well as the media in which the advertising is to be placed and defined advertising area, shall be at the discretion of the franchisor.

7. Trade Marks

A. Franchisor shall make available to franchisee franchisor's trade names and marks. For the purpose of this agreement, "the marks" shall be defined as all symbols, logos, trade marks, and trade names owned and/or under application by franchisor.

B. Franchisee agrees that its rights to use the marks are derived solely from this agreement, and franchisee shall not derive any right, title, or interest in the marks, other than a license to use them in connection with the franchise outlet while this agreement is in force,

C. Franchisee shall use the name and service marks only in such manner as prescribed by franchisor and in no other way.

D. Franchisee shall immediately notify franchisor of any apparent infringement of the use of the marks.

E. If it becomes advisable at any time in franchisor's sole discretion to discontinue or modify the use of any mark, franchisee agrees to comply within a reasonable time after notice thereof by franchisor.

8. Products, Supplies, and Equipment

Franchisee understands and acknowledges that every detail of the franchise system is important to franchisor, to franchisee, and to other franchises to develop and maintain high and uniform standards of quality, cleanliness, appearance, services, courses, and techniques, and to protect and enhance the reputation and goodwill of the franchise system. Franchisee accordingly agrees:

(1) To use all course materials, supplies, goods, signs, equipment, methods of exterior and interior design and construction, and methods of recruitment and instruction prescribed by or which conform to franchisor's standards and specifications.

(2) To refrain from using or offering any courses, materials, supplies, goods, signs, equipment, and methods of recruitment and instruction which do meet with franchisor's standards and specifications.

(3) To offer any such classes of products or services as shall be expressly approved for sale in writing by franchisor, and to offer all classes of products or services that have been designated as approved by franchisor.

(4) To purchase all products, supplies, equipment, and materials required for conduct of the franchise operation from suppliers who demonstrate, to the reasonable satisfaction of franchisor, the ability to meet all of franchisor's standards and specifications for such items; who possess adequate capacity and facilities to supply franchisee's needs in the quantities, at the times, and with the reliability requisite to an effective operation, and who have been approved, in writing, by the franchisor. Franchisee may submit to franchisor a written request for approval of a supplier not previously approved by franchisor.

9. Standards and Procedures

A. Management Standards

Franchisee agrees to comply with franchisor's standards with respect to products or services, customer solicitations, equipment, and facility maintenance, as documented in franchisor's Franchise Operating Manual for franchise outlets.

B. Personnel Standards

Franchisee shall hire only efficient, competent, sober, and courteous employees for the conduct of the business, and shall pay their wages, commissions, and other compensation with no liability thereof on the part of the franchisor. Franchisee shall require all employees to comply with franchisor's standards for grooming and appearance.

C. Best Efforts

Franchisee agrees to devote his/her best efforts to the operation of the outlet and to the supervision of its employees. Franchisee agrees that it will not engage in any other business activity which may conflict with the obligations of this agreement or impair the operation of the outlet.

D. Insurance

Franchisee shall, at his own expense, procure and maintain in full force and effect during the entire term of this agreement, comprehensive public, fire damage, product and motor vehicle liability insurance in the amount of One Million Dollars ($1,000,000) for each person and Three Million Dollars ($3,000,000) for each occurrence of bodily and personal injury, death and property damage. Fire damage insurance shall be sufficient to cover repair or replacement of all equipment, inventory, tools, and supplies normally required to operate the outlet, as specified in franchisor's operating manual. Franchisor shall be named as an additional insured under all such insurance policies, as its interests may appear, and contain a waiver by the carrier of all subrogation rights against franchisor. Maintenance of insurance under this paragraph shall not relieve franchisee of liability under the default provisions set forth in this agreement.

10. Training and Assistance

A. Franchisor agrees to provide personal training to franchisee, to furnish an operating manual, to make promotional and other recommendations, and to furnish franchisee, at franchisee's place of business, a qualified supervisor for not less than three (3) days during the initial six-day period of franchisee's operation.

B. Franchisor shall loan to franchisee for the term of this agreement an operating manual containing the standards, specifications, procedures, and techniques of the franchise system, and may, at its sole discretion, revise, from time to time, the contents of the manuals, incorporating new standards, specifications, procedures, and techniques.

C. Franchisor agrees to furnish franchisee with the following:

(1) guidelines and approval for the location of a suitable site for the outlet. By providing such guidelines and approval, franchisor in no way promises, warrants, or otherwise represents that the site location is the optimal location for the outlet;

(2) assistance in negotiating a lease for the outlet, when appropriate;

(3) assistance is planning the layout of the outlet;

(4) assistance in the conduct of a Grand Opening promotion for the outlet.

11. Business Conduct

A. All representations made by franchisee to others shall be completely factual. Franchisee agrees to abide by all laws, regulations, and codes.

B. Franchisee agrees to protect, defend, and indemnify franchisor and to hold franchisor harmless from and against any and all costs, expenses, including attorney's fees, court costs, losses, liabilities, damages, claims and demands of every kind or nature, arising in any way out of the occupation, use or operation, of any fixtures, equipment, goods, merchandise, or products used or sold at the outlet.

C. Franchisee will not divulge any business information, whether written or oral, received from franchisor or from any meetings of other of franchisor's franchisees, until such time as disclosure to the public may be required by the nature of the information. Such information may include, but is not limited to, promotional material or plans, expansion plans, new products, marketing information, costs or other financial data.

12. Inspections

A. Franchisor shall have the right to inspect franchisee's outlet and records, provided, however, that franchisee shall have been given reasonable advance notice. Franchisee agrees to cooperate fully with representatives of the franchisor making any such inspection.

13. Relationship of the Parties

A. Franchisee shall be an independent contractor, and nothing in this agreement shall be construed as to create or imply a fiduciary relationship between the parties, nor to make either party a general or specific agent, legal representative, subsidiary, joint venturer, or servant of the other.

B. Franchisee is in no way authorized to make a contract, agreement, warranty, or representation on behalf of franchisor to create any obligation, express or implied, on behalf of franchisor.

C. Franchisee shall be responsible for his/her own taxes, including without limitation any taxes levied upon the outlet.

14. Assignment of Franchise

Franchisee's rights in the franchise may be assigned only as follows:

A. Upon franchisee's death, the rights of franchisee in the franchise shall pass to franchisee's next of kin or other beneficiaries, provided that such next of kin or other beneficiaries shall agree in written form satisfactory to franchisor to assume all of franchisee's obligations under this agreement.

B. Franchisee may sell his interests in the franchise to another party, provided that the following conditions are met:

(1) The assignee is of good moral character, meets franchisor's normal qualifications for franchisees of franchisor, will comply with franchisor's training requirements, and enters into any and all direct agreements with franchisor that franchisor is then requiring of newly franchised persons.

(2) all monetary obligations of franchisee hereunder are fully paid, and franchisee executes a general release of all claims against franchisor, its officers, and directors;

(3) The assignee pays franchisor for its legal, training, and other expenses in connection with the assignment;

(4) franchisee has first offered to sell his franchise to franchisor upon the same terms as the purchaser has offered franchisee in writing, and franchisor has refused the offer or failed to accept it for a period of thirty (30) days;

(5) franchisee shall reaffirm a covenant not to compete in favor of franchisor;

C. Franchisee may assign and transfer his rights hereunder to a corporation without, however, being relieved of any personal liability, provided that the following conditions are met:

(1) the corporation is newly formed and shall conduct no other business but the franchise business, which shall continue to be managed by franchisee;

(2) franchisee owns the controlling stock interest in the corporation and is the principal executive officer thereof;

(3) the articles of incorporation, by-laws and other organizational documents of the corporation shall recite that the issuance and assignment of any interest therein is restricted by the terms of this agreement, and all issued and outstanding stock certificates of such corporation shall bear a legend reflecting or referring to the restrictions of this agreement;

(4) all stockholders of the corporation guarantee, in written form satisfactory to franchisor, to be bound jointly and severally by all provisions of this franchise agreement;

(5) franchisee shall not use any mark in a public offering of his securities, except to reflect his franchise relationship with franchisor.

15. Termination

If franchisee defaults under the terms of this agreement and such default shall not be cured within thirty (30) days after receipt of written notice to cure from franchisor, then, in addition to all other remedies at law or in equity, franchisor may immediately terminate this agreement. Termination under such conditions shall become effective immediately upon receipt by franchisee of a written notice of termination. Franchisee shall be considered to be in default under this agreement if:

(1) franchisee fails to open the business within the time specified in Section 4 of this agreement;

(2) franchisee abandons the franchise;

(3) franchisee attempts to assign this agreement without prior written approval of franchisor;

(4) franchisee misuses or makes an unauthorized use of the mark in a manner which materially impairs the goodwill of the franchisor;

(5) franchisee has made a material misrepresentation to franchisor before and after being granted the franchise;

(6) franchisee discloses or reproduces any portion of the franchisor's operating manual to any unauthorized party;

(7) franchisee fails to abide by his covenant not to compete as provided in this agreement;

(8) franchisee fails to comply substantially with any of the requirements imposed upon franchisee by this agreement.

16. Rights and Obligations of the Parties Upon Termination or Expiration

A. On termination or expiration of this agreement, franchisee shall do or cause to be done the following:

(1) promptly pay all amounts owed to franchisor which are then unpaid;

(2) immediately cease to use any and all marks and names, and any other trade secrets, confidential information, operating manuals, slogans, signs, symbols, or devices forming part of the franchise system or otherwise used in connection with conduct of the franchise outlet.

(3) immediately return to franchisor all advertising materials, operating manuals, plans, specifications, and other materials prepared by franchisor and relative to the franchise system.

B. Covenant not to compete

Franchisee, its officers, directors, and shareholders agree during the term of this agreement, or upon expiration or termination, or nonrenewal for any reason, they shall not have any interest as an owner, partner, director, officer, employee, manager, consultant, shareholder, representative, agent, or in any other capacity for any reason for a period of two (2) years after the occurrence of said events in any business or activity involving the conduct of a proprietary post-secondary educational institution or training school or program, or proposing to engage in the conduct of a proprietary post-secondary educational institution or training school or program, except with the written permission of franchisor.

Franchisee acknowledges that this covenant is reasonable and necessary and agrees that its failure to adhere strictly to the restrictions of this paragraph will cause substantial and irreparable damage to franchisor. Franchisee hereby acknowledges, therefore, that any violation of the terms and conditions of this covenant shall give rise to an entitlement to injunctive relief.

17. Enforcement and Construction

A. Severability

The paragraphs of this agreement are severable, and in the event any paragraph or portion of the agreement is declared illegal or unenforceable, the remainder of the agreement shall be effective and binding on the parties.

B. Notice

Whenever, under the terms of this agreement, notice is required, the same shall be deemed delivered if delivered by hand to whom intended, or to any adult person employed by franchisee at franchisee's place of business, or upon deposit in any U.S. depository for mail delivery, addressed to franchisee or franchisor at their respective business addresses.

C. Specific performance.

Nothing contained herein shall bar the franchisor's or franchisee's right to obtain specific performance of the provisions of this agreement and injunctive relief against threatened conduct that will cause it loss or damages, under customary equity rules, including applicable rules for obtaining retraining orders and preliminary injunctions.

D. Governing law

This agreement is entered into and shall be construed in accordance with the laws of the state of Arizona, as of the date of execution of this agreement.

E. Successors

This agreement shall inure to the benefit of and be binding upon the executors, administrators, heirs, assigns and successors in interest of the parties.

APPENDIX B

FRANCHISEE RESOURCES

American Arbitration Association
Washington, DC Regional Office
1120 Connecticut Avenue NW, Suite 490
Washington, DC 20036
(202) 223-7093
www.adr.org

American Association of Franchisees and Dealers
P.O. Box 10158
Palm Desert, CA 92255-1058
800-733-9858
www.aafd.org

American Bar Association Forum on Franchising
321 North Clark Street
Chicago, IL 60654-7598
americanbar.org

Association for Conflict Resolution
1639 Bradley Park Dr., Suite 500-142
Columbus, GA 31904
(202) 780-5999
www.acrnet.org

California Department of Business Oversight
1515 K Street, Suite 200
Sacramento, CA 95814-4052
(866) 275-2677
dbo.ca.gov

Federal Trade Commission
600 Pennsylvania Avenue NW
Washington, DC 20580
Telephone: (202) 326-2222
www.ftc.gov

Hawaii Department of Commerce and Consumer Affairs
Securities Compliance Branch
335 Merchant Street, Room 205
Honolulu, HI 96813
(808) 586-2722
cca.hawaii.gov/sec

Illinois Attorney General's Office
Franchise Bureau
500 South Second Street
Springfield, IL 62706
(217) 782 – 4465
www.illinoisattorneygeneral.gov

Indiana Secretary of State
Securities Division
302 West Washington Street, Room E-111
Indianapolis, IN 46204
(317) 232-6681
www.in.gov/sos/securities

Maryland Office of Attorney General
Securities Division
200 St. Paul Place, 20th Floor
Baltimore, MD 21202
(410) 576-6300
www.marylandattorneygeneral.gov

Michigan Department of Attorney General
Consumer Protection Division
PO Box 30213
Lansing, MI 48909
(517) 373-7117
www.michigan.gov/ag

Minnesota Department of Commerce
Franchise Division
133 East 7th Street
St. Paul, MN 55101
(651) 296-6328
www.mn.gov/commerce

Minority Business Development Agency
10750 Columbia Pike
Suite 200
Silver Spring, MD 20901
(301) 242-5320
www.mbda.gov

National Federation of Independent Businesses
1201 F St, NW (btw 12th & 13th St)
Washington, D.C. 20004
(202) 554-9000
www.nfib.com

New York State Department of Law
120 Broadway, 23rd Floor
New York, NY 10271
(212) 416-8211
www.ag.ny.gov

North Dakota Securities Department
Franchise Division
600 East Boulevard, 5th Floor
Bismarck, ND 58505
(701) 328-2910
www.nd.gov/securities

Office of the National Ombudsman
409 3rd Street, S.W. Suite 7125
Washington, DC 20416
888-734-3247
www.sba.gov/ombudsman

Rhode Island Department of Business Regulation
1511 Pontiac
Cranston, RI 02920
(410) 462-9500
www.dbr.state.ri.us

U.S. Department of Justice
ADA Mediation Program
950 Pennsylvania Avenue, NW
Washington, D.C. 20530
(202) 307-0663
www.ada.gov

U.S. Small Business Administration
409 3rd St, SW
Washington DC 20416
800-827-5722
www.sba.gov

Virginia State Corporation Commission
1300 E Main St
Richmond, VA 23219
(804) 371-9733
www.scc.virginia.gov

Washington State Department of Financial Institutions
P.O. Box 9033
Olympia, WA 98507
(360) 902-8760
dfi.wa.gov

Wisconsin State Department of Financial Institutions
201 W Washington Ave
Madison, WI 53703
(608) 261-9555
www.wdfi.org

INDEX

advertisements, franchisee recruitment, 113
advertising
 fees, 67-68
 royalties, 68
 system, 50, 67, 190
AI, see artificial intelligence
Alabama franchise statutes, 136
Amended Franchise Rule, 74, 80, 89-90
America's Favorite Chicken Company, Inc., 20
American Society for Training and Development (ASTD), 161
application for franchise, 122
arbitration, 138-139, 148, 151
area franchising, 71-72
Aristotle, 29
artificial intelligence (AI), 153
artificial neural networks (ANNs), 155
assignment, 191
assistance, franchisor, 50
attitudes, extroverted and introverted, 29-30
audits, 133-134, 190
authorization to advertise, 85-86

Bagram Air Field, 5
bankruptcy history, 76, 85-96
Big Data, 156
blueprints, 49
Bora Bora, 6
Brown, Graham, 139
Burger King, 5, 12, 53, 57, 135

business experience, disclosure requirement, 92
business format, 46, 47
business opportunities, 56
business organization, 197-202
buying decisions
 complex, 111
 cultural influences, 116
 low involvement, 116

Cafua, Mark, 20-21
California Department of Corporations, 82
California Franchise Investment Protection Law, 23
cast reserves, importance of, 167
civil actions, 166
Coca-Cola, 18
comfort, physiology of, 9-10
complex buying decisions, 111
computer systems, 100
control of ownership, 200
cooperative advertising, 7, 44, 50, 67
Coors Brewery v. U.S. Federal Trade Commission (law case), 135
Copeland Enterprises, Inc., 20
Copeland, Aaron, 19-20
copyrights, 103
corporate documents, 201
corporations, 199
cultural influences in buying decisions, 116
cybercrime, 159

data breaches, 159-161
data mining, 156-157

demographic cliff, 12, 222
demographics, 32
  of business owners, 32-34
  of franchisees, 33
designs, 49
development and improvement, 186-187, 203
Dickey's Barbecue Restaurants, Inc. v. Chorley Enterprises, Inc. (legal case), 86
disclosure document, see Franchise Disclosure Document
disclosure requirements, 75, 76
discomfort zones, 10
dispute resolution, 104-105, 146
Docktor Pet, 137
Dunkin' Donuts, 21

e-commerce, impact of, 215-216
earnings estimate, 105-106, 173
empirical data, 114
estimated initial investment, 97
evaluating franchise fees, 72
exclusivity, 62
exemptions to franchise regulations, 46, 81
exit strategy, 177
expulsions from security associations, 166

false urgency, 79
FDD, see Franchise Disclosure Document
federal franchise regulations, 73, 80
Federal Franchise Rule, 24
Federal Trade Commission Act, 73
fee impoundment, 85
Fees, 45, 53, 58, 64, 96, 174, 184-185
  advertising, 67-68

financial performance, 105-106
financial stability, importance of, 167
financing, disclosure requirement, 100
fixtures and improvements, 203
format, business, 46, 47
franchise agreement, 106, 138, 139, 181-196
franchise application form, 122
franchise categories, 16
Franchise Disclosure Document, (FDD) 24, 51, 80, 89-107, 125, 146
  sample cover page, 78
franchise disputes, 129, 141-150
franchise escrow account, 85
franchise fees, 45, 53, 58, 64, 72, 96, 174, 184-185
  evaluating, 72
franchise information kit, 119-120
franchise operating manual, 44, 49, 52, 53, 206-210
franchise outlets, 106
  lowest performing, 14
franchise recruitment ads, 113
franchise registration, 84
franchise relationship, 41, 184
franchise royalties, 53, 64
Franchise Rule, 74, 80, 89-90
  exemptions, 81
franchise semantics, 56
franchise territory, 102, 175-176
franchise ultrastructure, 70
franchise, assignment of, 191
franchise, definition, 7, 17, 42, 47
franchise, legal definition, 42
franchise operated as a corporation, 199-201

251

franchise regulations, 22, 23, 25, 73, 82-86, 225-226
franchise success rate, 7-8
franchise trademark, 18
franchisee identity, 47
franchisee obligations, 130-134
franchisee recruitment, 119
franchisee reports, 131-133
franchisee rights, 134-135
franchisee, definition, 18
franchisee, expectations, 21
franchisee, obligations, 99
franchisees, existing, 106, 172
franchisees, traits of, 34
franchises, gross annual sales, 14
franchising and the economy, 13
franchising and the law, 8
franchisor assistance, 50, 76, 100
franchisor viability index, 178
franchisor's computer systems, 100
FTC, see U.S. Federal Trade Commission

goodwill
  definition of, 59-60
  value of, 59-60
Google analytics, 158
governing law, 196
grant of franchise, 181
grooming of employees, 133

Hertz, 6, 42
Hippocrates, 28
House Committee of Small Business, 129

identity, 50
IFA, see International Franchise Association
Illinois Franchise Disclosure Act, 83

image and conduct, 188
impoundment of initial fee, 85
incentives, promotional, 58
information processing, 112
initial fee, 45, 53, 58-64, 96, 174
initial fees, disclosure requirement, 96
initial investment, 33, 57, 68-69, 97
insolvency, 213
inspections and audits, 133-134
Intelligent Tutoring Systems (ITS), 161
International Franchise Association, 25, 47, 139
Investment, 57, 68-69
Iowa Franchise Relationship Law, 24

Jung, Carl, 28-30

KFC, 5, 41
lead processing, 119
length of time in business, 165
liability, vicarious, 137
litigation, 149, 166
  disclosure of, 94
management changes, 132
market, value of, 61-62
Maryland Franchise Law, 86
McDonald's, 5, 12, 13-14, 42, 53, 137
mediation, 147
multi-unit operators, 33
multi-unit performance, 54

need arousal, 112

obligation to participate in operation of business, 104
occupations most at risk of automation (chart), 164

ongoing fees, 64
operating statement, 132
operating system, 46, 49, 186
operations manual, 44, 49, 52, 53, 175, 206-210
outlet development, 186-187
outlet maintenance, 133
ownership changes, 132
ownership, control of, 200

Paris, France, 5
partnerships, 199
patents, 103
Patterson v. Domino's Pizza, LLC (law case), 137
payments, 45-47, 53
personal guarantee, 201
Popeye's, 19, 20
population shift, impact of, 215, 220-223
predecessors, disclosure requirement, 91
premises, security, 202
price fixing, 135
Princeton University, 158
Principe v. McDonald's Corp. (law case), 137
product specifications, 49
products and services, restrictions on, 98, 104
promotional incentives, 58
proprietary information, 103
psychological Types, 28
psychometrics, 28, 30
public figures, 171
  disclosure requirement, 105
purchasing standards, 99

quality standards, 138

Ramada Inns v. Gadsden Motel Co. (law case), 138

receipts, for initial payments, 107
reference groups, 117
registration states, 23, 82
renewal, 104-105, 193
reports and audits, 190-191
rescission, right of, 79
restrictions on products and services, 98, 104, 176-177
Return on Investment (ROI), 54-55
reverse selling, 111
right of rescission, 79
robots in the workplace, 162
royalties
  advertising, 68
  franchise, 53

sales projections, 105-106, 173
security associations, 166
security, 159-161
7-Eleven Stores, 22, 42
severability, 195
sharing economy, 216, 223-224
Siegel v. Chicken Delight (law case), 136
significant control or assistance, 43-45, 52
site selection, 44, 202-203
  fee, 97
skill sets, 30-31, 38-39
sole proprietorship, 198-199
Southland Corporation, 22
Starbuck's, 41
start-up investment, 33
state regulation of franchises, 82-86
state vs. federal regulations, 86
stock legends, 201
stock market vulnerability, 55
Stuller, Inc. v. Steak N Shake Enterprises, Inc. (law case), 135

subfranchisor, 69-70
substitution clause, 195
Subway, 41
super consumer generation, impact of, 12, 221-223
symbiotic relationships, 17
system, operating, 46, 49

tax considerations, 198
technology, impact on franchising, 153-164
termination, 104-105, 194, 195
territorial restrictions, 44
territory, 102, 175-176, 212
   exclusive, 62
   value of, 59, 61, 70
tie-in arrangements, 136-137
time for making of disclosures, 77
trade name, 46, 50
trade name franchising, 72
trademark, 42-43, 48, 50-51, 102-103, 133, 171, 182-183
   infringements, 133
   registration, 50-51
training cost, 59, 100, 173
training program, 47, 48-49, 100, 167, 173, 174-175, 185
traits of successful franchisees, 34

U.S. Census Bureau, 32
U.S. Department of Commerce, 7, 14
U.S. Federal Trade Commission, 9, 23, 44, 54, 73
U.S. Patent and Trademark Office, 51
U.S. Small Business Administration, 23
U.S. v. Parke Davis & Co. (law case), 135
ultrastructure, 70
Uniform Franchise Offering Circular (UFOC), 82
updates, requirement, 86

vicarious liability, 137

Wall Street Journal, 9, 113
Wendy's, 5, 12
Wilson, Woodrow, 74
working capital, 98, 214
workout process, 147
World Economic Forum (WEF), 162
Wyndham Worldwide, 160

Zoning, 202

ABOUT THE AUTHOR

Dennis L. Foster is regarded as one of America's foremost authorities on franchising, finance, and marketing. Actively involved in franchise development and deployment for over 40 years, he has written more than 60 published books on franchising, finance, technology, health care, sociology, and communications. His biography, interviews, quotations, and books about franchising have been featured in such publications as *USA Today, Business Week, U.S. News and World Reports, The Kiplinger Report, Business Digest,* and *Computer World*.

www.ingramcontent.com/pod-product-compliance
Lightning Source LLC
Chambersburg PA
CBHW021353210526
45463CB00001B/94